D1516330

THE PURSUIT

THE
PURSUIT

EXPLORING THE HEART OF GOD

JOSHUA FREEMAN

 START2FINISH

© 2016 by Joshua Freeman

All rights reserved. No part of this publication may be reproduced, stored in a re-
trieval system, or transmitted in any form or by any means without the prior written
permission of the author. The only exception is brief quotations in printed reviews.

ISBN-10: 1944704302
ISBN-13: 978-1944704308

Published by Start2Finish
Fort Worth, Texas 76244
www.start2finish.org

Printed in the United States of America

Unless otherwise noted, all Scripture quotations are from The Holy Bible, English
Standard Version®, copyright © 2001 by Crossway Bibles, a publishing ministry
of Good News Publishers. Used by permission. All rights reserved.

Cover Design: Josh Feit, Evangela.com

CONTENTS

INTRODUCTION

Three preachers were in a coffee shop discussing the moment when life begins. One preacher said, "Life begins when the child takes his or her first breath." Another said, "No, it begins when the child is conceived." The last preacher interrupted, "You both have it wrong! Life begins when the last child leaves home, and the dog finally dies!"

There are a variety of views about when life really begins. As a child, you believe it begins at 13, then later when you can drive at 16, or surely when you can move out at the age of 18. No matter what age or moment you see as the beginning of "living life," we all pursue it. So many dreams are pursued that are not life fulfilling today. The American dream of a home fit for HGTV, two beautiful cars, lots of money, and a great family has taken the front seat in many lives. Parents pursue sports and academic scholarship for their children as they put everything else aside. The one thing we often don't consider pursuing and end up neglecting is God.

MY INTENTIONS FOR THIS BOOK

It is my hope that this book will help the reader better understand and share the pursuit of God. By providing a brief, thirteen-chapter overview of pursuing God, the reader will then be able to guide others through the evangelistic study found in Appendix B. While the book is intended to provide a wider scope of understanding, it can also be used as a class or small group course. Appendix A provides helpful study tips and an outline of the Pursuing God Discipleship Study for those just beginning their journey. This section offers some introductory advice and an outline for the disciple to consider before beginning the study with a student. Appendix B is the study that a non-Christian, or a new Christian would participate in. It is a study that can be self-guided or, as I prefer, discussed in a weekly meeting of three to five seekers.

This guide will provide insight, depth, and breadth to self-guided students, Christians who don't know where to begin studying with a seeker, or mature Christians who just want to try a new approach. This approach stands on the shoulders of many giants of the faith. While most approaches use similar verses, the presentation of this approach is intended to help an individual fall in love with God so that they may begin pursuing the God who already pursues them. As a minister, this book is the first discipleship study I take an individual through in his or her quest to learn more about God and begin journeying towards him. All Bible verses are taken out of the English Standard Version unless otherwise noted.

THE NEED FOR THIS MATERIAL

I was sitting in my office one day when Sam, a member of our congregation, called me for a consultation. Sam was a deacon in the congregation who had grown up attending church every time the doors were opened. He had heard countless sermons on the love and grace of God but struggled to organize his thoughts on the subject when discussing it with others. On this day, Sam was approached by a friend who knew the religious nature of his life. Seizing the opportunity to share the overall story of God, Sam invited his friend to meet with him and learn more about who God is and what he asks of us. Eager to learn more, his friend accepted the invitation and left Sam searching for a starting point. As Sam explained his dilemma, he asked where he should begin. I suggested he begin by exploring the love and intentions of a pursuing God with his friend.

Many Christians may be able to declare the reason they followed God but struggle to teach those reasons to others. They may even know someone who would like to know more about God, but they need a starting point to help begin such an important discussion with their friend. This exploration of God's love and intentions gives both a starting point and a broad overview of the larger story of the pursuing God throughout history. In a time where more and more are struggling to understand God, this material is vital to the growth of his kingdom. It provides a starting point for the Christian who wants to lead a Bible study and a guide for those desiring to learn about the narrative of God.

MY PRAYER FOR THE READER

I pray that God will bless your efforts as you seek him and point another towards him. This study has blessed many lives and has led many to pursue God. Knowing this, I am certain of God's blessing however this book is used. Although we plant and water the seed, it is God who gives the growth. My prayer is that God will allow this material to plant a seed in you and those you meet so that he can provide a plentiful harvest (Matt. 9:37)!

CHAPTER ONE

THE CREATIVE GOD

GENESIS 1

I'll never forget the birth of my first child. Even before her birth, my wife and I shared many special, wonderful moments in preparing for her arrival. The cold air and several feet of snow, common during an upstate New York January, weren't going to keep us from the appointment to hear and see our baby for the first time. Walking into the doctor's office, we could hardly contain ourselves. "We get to see our child today," my wife joyfully exclaimed. As we sat in the waiting room, the excitement began to grow as the minutes began to feel like hours. Finally, a door opened and the nurse called our name. Leaping out of our seats, we scurried into the hallway and through the office door. There is nothing like the sense of joy experienced from seeing your child's heart beat and hearing its pitter-patter for the first time. Over the next several months, our child continued to develop into a healthy little girl. The day this gift from God was delivered, our lives changed forever. Holding my daughter for the first time, I knew that she was perfect in every way. The moment she lay in my arms was the moment I knew that there was nothing that could ever take my love from her. We belonged with each other. In my eyes, she was perfect.

She will, as children do, continue to grow and mature. She will have good days and bad days. She will make good choices and poor choices. There will be days of joy and sorrow for her, but she will always be mine. She will always be her daddy's little girl no matter what life brings. The perfection I saw the first time I held her will be the perfection I will see every time I look into her eyes. I know she will make mistakes. I know there will be times her mother and I don't know what to do, but I know that my love for her will continually grow stronger each day.

Most parents can identify with these feelings of holding their child for the first time. The feelings of joy, excitement, and unexplainable joy are a precious part of parenthood. But human parents are not the only ones who experience these wonderful feelings. God, our creator and father, feels this way as well. It was not only the natural world and beasts of the air and sea that God created, he also created humanity. In Genesis 1:26 we see God's desire to create humans who would bear his likeness. This special creation, humanity, would rule over every other creature on earth and would go about the work of its father. Just as we bear a resemblance to our earthly fathers, we exhibit a resemblance to our creator, the God of Heaven and Earth (Gen. 1:27). Made in his image, we function as reminders of this God's artistic design.

THE GIFT OF CREATIVITY

There are a variety of ways one can be creative. Some people can take an ordinary object and turn it into a masterpiece, while others can create art from nothing. My creativity and artistic side begins and ends in music, but this is not the case for the rest of my family. I have a sister, father, grandmother, grandfather, aunt, and several cousins who are very artistic, especially in the visual arts field. Some are able to see a masterpiece in a blank canvas while others can see the beauty that lies beneath a stump of wood or lump of clay. Within these materials something seems to call out to them and appear, as if by magic, before their eyes. There is no doubt that God has gifted them with artistic creativity.

Creativity, especially when involving the visual arts, is highly valued in today's society. Art museums are no longer located only in the downtown districts of major cities, but are scattered in even some of the smallest of towns. Entrepreneurs desiring to sell their products will spend a significant portion of their budget on artistic marketing campaigns that merge creativity and the product pitch. They understand the importance of connecting their brand with the artistic interest of their consumers. They seek to create a connection between the company, product, and purchaser.

God, in many ways, is not so different from the creative artists of today. At the beginning of Genesis, God creates a masterpiece out of both a blank canvas and a world in chaos. The creative God is able to see the beautiful masterpiece found within the lump of clay. He sees a masterpiece so magnificent that even God, himself, marvels at its unveiling.

THE CREATION

"In the beginning, God created…"(Gen. 1:1). The idea of creation has always perplexed me. You have a God who has everything he could ever want and need. In the unlikely event that it does not yet exist, God is able to easily create it out of thin air. This ever active God chose to tap into his artistic form and create. The opening verses of Genesis paint a bleak picture. The earth is created but is formless, dark, and filled with water. Earth appears to be in a state of chaos. There is nothing formed, nothing set in order, and nothing to be excited about. It is in the midst of this dark ball of chaos that we find the creative God at work. Unafraid of the challenge, the creative God begins the work of putting order to the chaos. He created light and separated it from the darkness, giving the earth day and night on the first day. From this point on it gets more complex. The creation of day and night is followed by creation of the sky and dry land on the second and third days. On the fourth day, vegetation among the dry ground along with the stars and planets we see in space were formed.

These amazing creations of the first four days were only the beginning of

God's creative work. Day five springs forth the creatures of the sea and air as life becomes even more complex and intricate. Upon the dry ground, God will begin the sixth day with his creation of all the living animals upon the earth. The last day, however, God demonstrates not only his most magnificent creativity, but also his most prized creation—humanity.

GOD'S DELIGHT IN CREATION

At the completion of God's creative masterpiece, Genesis 1:28 says that he blessed the man and woman. Wow! Out of all creation, it is humanity that God blesses! The man and woman were directed to procreate and rule over the rest of creation. The blessing of God was of great importance to the health of both humanity and the rest of creation. It signified God's pleasure in them.

The love the father has for his creation is also evidenced by this blessing. Just as parents desire to bless their children, our father desires to bless his children, humanity, as well. Jesus emphasizes this point when he says, "If you then, who are evil, know how to give good gifts to your children, how much more will your Father who is in heaven give good things to those who ask him!" (Matt. 7:11).

It is important to understand that a blessing does not occur without stipulations and limitations. For example, God desires for us to ask for his help and blessings from time to time (Jer. 6:16; Matt. 11:28-30). As we will see throughout our study, blessings can be modified by God, dependent upon our obedience and proximity to him. Freedom of choice accompanies the blessings of God; however, poor choices can hinder the blessings of God in our lives (Isa.59:1-2).

The phrase "God saw that it was good" occurs seven times throughout the first chapter of Genesis. Each major section of creation finishes with the approval of God using the term "good." In fact, once humanity is created in the image of God, the creative work of God becomes not just good, but very good. The artist stands at the end of the sixth day pleased with his masterpiece.

A COMPETING IMAGE

Throughout history God has been portrayed as one who is on a mission to make us pay for our sins, as if he sits on a cloud waiting to strike us down with lightning. He is seen as a God who takes pleasure in persecution and destruction. In fact, God is often seen as rooting against his creation rather than for it, as if he is ashamed and displeased. The brutal and narcissistic Greco-Roman gods have more in common with this false idea many have of God than how the first chapter of Genesis presents him to us. The chronicle of creation depicts a creative God who loves his work. He is an artist who looks at his masterpiece and says, "it is very good." And why wouldn't he? After all, his masterpiece was created in his own image and given his very breath of life!

Nowhere in the creation account, or the rest of scripture, does it teach that humanity was created sinful. The Bible never states that any of God's creation was evil. If this were the case, God would cease to be God since he is good and that which is good cannot create evil. Instead of an evil creation, we see that God's creation exceeded expectations. His masterpiece is deeply loved as a father loves his child.

It is tempting to blame our shortcomings on someone else rather than take responsibility for our actions. This is why so many try to place the blame on God, as if he messed up his canvas. God, the creative artist, cannot help but create perfection. When that masterpiece ceases to be good, it is not because of God, but because the masterpiece is not being who it was created to be. It is not following its artist. However, when the masterpiece of God fulfills its purpose, it will bring praise to its creator as a canvas to its painter.

So, how can God's masterpiece cease to reflect the creative artist? It is to this discussion we will turn next. For now, it is imperative to understand that you are created in the very image of God, as his masterpiece, and have been given his very breath. You were created "very good."

SUMMARY

- You were created "very good."

QUESTIONS

1. What stood out to you in Genesis 1?

2. Is there a way people inside the church tend to view God? Is this view different for people outside the church?

3. How have your views of God changed throughout the course of your life?

4. What does it mean to be created in the image of someone? What does it mean to be created in the image of God? How is this significant?

5. Why do you think it was important for the writer to point out that God blessed humanity?

6. What insight or actions do these passages teach you to implement?

CHAPTER TWO

THE LOVING GOD

GENESIS 2

W hile the first chapter of Genesis gives a panoramic view of creation, Genesis two focuses on the creation of humanity. Chapter two's narrow focus illustrates the importance of the creation of humans and their special relationship with their creator. From the dust of the ground, the creative God formed man and breathed life into him. Giving him the task of caring for the Garden of Eden and naming the animals, God blessed him with food that was not only pleasant to look at, but was also good to eat.

Why did God do all of this? Irenaeus, an early church father from the second century, taught that God formed Adam, not because he had a need of man, but because he desired to bless someone. The God who had everything desired to share it with another being! He did not stop with the creation of Adam. In wisdom, the creative God noticed that it was not good for Adam to be alone, so he set his mind to make a helper for Adam. During a deep sleep and from a rib of Adam, God created him a helper, a woman named Eve (Gen. 2:20). Eve would live alongside Adam in the garden as they tended to the plants, worked with the animals, and ate freely of the produce. A special tree was placed in the middle of the garden—the tree of life. This was a tree that promised sustenance and longevity of life; a tree that guaranteed the physical well-being of God's masterpiece. God also planted a tree called "The Knowledge of Good and Evil." Eden's lush landscape was beautiful and practical. It was paradise, a place where God walked among his creation.

THE PROVISION OF A GOOD FATHER

Throughout his creative process, God demonstrated his love and provision for the needs of Adam. Humanity was not created and left to fend for itself. The Creator did not merely make Adam and walk away. He loved and cared for his masterpiece by providing him with food, water, and companionship. In the book of Luke, Jesus illustrates the provision and love of God that is seen in both creation and the current era. Jesus identifies the behavior of a good father with that of the heavenly father. Just as a good father looks after the wellbeing and health of his child, the heavenly father provides the same care for you and me out of love (Luke 11:11-13).

Provision takes place in many ways. Years ago as an adolescent, my twin brother and I went on a Boy Scout retreat with my dad. The camp was located in beautiful northwest New Mexico. Trees, hills, and water painted the landscape. A lake for swimming, boating, fishing, and other recreational activities was located at the south end of the camp beyond the descent of a large hill. Excited to jump into the cool water, the three of us put on our swim trunks and hurried down to the lake with the rest of the group. As the afternoon progressed, dark clouds and thunder quickly began to roll in from the west. The dark blue-grey sky was beautiful, but threatened the potential of lightning, so we exited the lake and began to gather our things.

Suddenly, a park ranger's truck slid to a halt on the gravel as he called my dad and other adults over. The sky was turning from beautiful blue-grey to an eerie green-grey, and my father ran over to hurry us up the hill to the mess hall. This was the day I learned what a wall-cloud looked like. As we hurried up the hill, rain and nickel sized hail began to beat upon us. With still a long way to go, our tent was the nearest safety we could reach. Sirens began to blare and the wind began to howl as we approached the tent. Tying the canvas of the pup-tent entry together, my dad instructed my brother and I to get under the cot and take cover. We crammed together under the cot, and my father squeezed under as best he could and instructed us to grab onto the protective canvas. As the wind whipped and tore the tent from the wooden foundation, dad grabbed it with his hand to hold it over us. Those few moments were possibly the most terrifying moments of my childhood. We were lucky to escape the nearby tornado with only a few cuts and bruises. The love my father had for us led him to provide for our safety above his own. Not only did my father provide food, clothing, and shelter, he also provided security in the midst of chaos. All my life my father has provided for the needs of his family. Our loving God is no different. Because of his great love for us, God provided humanity with everything we need to be secure, sustained, and healthy.

Looking back to the beginning, we see how God always provided for his creation—especially humanity. He provided humanity with items of such interest that we can't help but marvel at his brilliance. He could have allowed Adam to work the garden alone, but he instead provided a helper for him to work alongside and tend to creation. Rather than sending Adam scouring for food, God provided a lush garden filled with everything he could ever desire to eat and rivers of fresh, clean water were created to irrigate the garden and refresh the gardeners.

GOD PROVIDED A CHOICE

Did God create sin? Why would the creative God place a beautiful tree among the garden and instruct Adam and Eve not to eat of its fruit? Would a loving God create something and then ask us to not enjoy it? What kind of cruel being would tempt his child to disobey him? These questions, and many more, are often asked when looking at the second chapter of Genesis. Within the garden, God placed a forbidden tree, and he instructed humanity not to eat of this tree. In fact, God tells them, "You may eat of every tree of the garden, but of the tree of the knowledge of good and evil you shall not eat, for in the day you eat of it you will die" (Gen. 2:16-17). In planting this tree in Eden, God did not create sin and temptation. Certainly the tree was not there to put Adam and Eve to the test. Rather, it is a beautiful representation of our loving God's provision of choice. God did not want to force us to love him; rather, he desires that we choose to love him from our own free will. To love God out of our free will is to obey his requests (1 John 5:3).

In the previous chapter I told the story of my first child's birth, the love I have for her, and the love I hope she will always have for me. I pray and hope that throughout her life she will choose to love me out of her own free will. If you think about it, that is what each of us desires. A spouse, parent, child, friend, or coworker—whoever it is, we hope that they, by their own initiative, choose to love us, befriend us, and desire to be near us. Forced friendship is really no friendship at all. Love that is demanded is not love—it is a burden. Of all his creation, God desired a special relationship with humanity. He loved those who received his breath, and his desire is for us to reciprocate that love, but God will never force you to love him.

God understands that forced love and allegiance is not from the heart. God desires love and allegiance of our free will. It is the seeking after him with all of our being because of our love for him that speaks to our creator. This pursuit of God softens his heart as he is touched by our choice. Children have a way of melting our hearts. My arrival home is often greeted by a little girl running as fast as possible across the house towards me as she calls out, "Daddy, Daddy, Daddy!" I am met with a tackling hug and lots of kisses. Holding my hand, she leads me to where she is playing and offers me a toy, piece of cereal, dog bone, or whatever she is currently playing with. Her eyes, words, and actions speak one simple truth—she has chosen to love me.

GOD CHOSE TO LOVE YOU

Our creator chooses to love you. In fact, he chases after you and longs to have a relationship with you. Just as God pursues you, he desires for you to have a choice in loving him. In fact, Genesis 2:16-17 teaches that God did not force Adam and Eve to choose him—he gave them a way out! God understands that forced love is really no love. God actually designed free will, the freedom to choose, from the first moment of humanity's existence in hopes you would choose him. This demonstrates the vulnerability of God

The ultimate question God asks is, "What and who will you choose?" Our creator wants to know if you will choose him or yourself. He wants to know if you will obey him or another. Will you trust the creator God or will you trust another god? God's love for you is preeminent and continues regardless of your choice. No matter what you do, he loves you deeply, but he has made clear that his provision and blessing are contingent upon the choice you make. God will provide what you need, but you must freely seek him out of your own decision and desire to love him. If you choose God, you will receive his provision and blessing.

None can fully understand the mind of God, but we can understand his love and compassion by observing the details of creation. If we understand God's love and compassion, we will realize that he is unable to create anything that is not good. This means that God's creation, especially humanity, is good at its very core. Humanity is loved by its creator and given the free-will to reciprocate that love. This free-will choice is demonstrated between the choice of good and evil. If we desire good, we must continually choose God and keep in step with him. The loving God will provide for the needs of those who choose him. After all, he loves you!

SUMMARY

- You were created "very good."
- God loves you enough to let you choose.

QUESTIONS

1. What stood out to you in Genesis 2?

2. How does God provide for the needs of his creation?

3. What is the significance of our freedom of choice?

4. What actions does this passage call you to implement in your life?

5. How did God view humanity in the beginning?

6. What does this chapter teach you about the purity of humanity at this point?

CHAPTER THREE

THE BETRAYED GOD

GENESIS 3

The year 1599 brought with it a story that would impact the literary world and students in literature classes for the next several hundred years. In this year, William Shakespeare completed his famous play *The Tragedy of Julius Caesar*. Although named after Caesar, this play is more about Marcus Brutus than it is about the emperor of Rome. Brutus struggles throughout the play with loyalty to his friend. Fearing what might happen to Rome if Caesar were to accept the crown, many began to plot against him and sought to enlist the help and approval of Brutus. By the third act of the play, Brutus decided it was in the best interest of Rome to put an end to the life of his confidant. As Casca, a co-conspirator, gains close quarters with Caesar, he signals the group who begins stabbing the war hero. Brutus is the last to plunge a knife into his back. As the bleeding emperor looks upon his murderers and identifies Brutus, he finds enough breath to acknowledge his betrayal in his famous line, "And you also Brutus?"

Can you imagine the pain of Caesar's betrayal? Shakespeare adds that the ruler lost his will to live after being betrayed by his close friend. You might say it was a broken heart that ultimately took his life rather than the knife wounds. How would you feel if a loved one betrayed you? We have all likely felt the betrayal of a loved one, a close friend, or trusted ally. Our struggle with betrayal is shared with God who would be betrayed by his creation.

PLAYING GOD

There is no telling how much time has passed between the creation of Adam and Eve and Genesis 3. A new character simply identified as the serpent enters into the scene. This serpent was considered to be the craftiest creature of the land and taunts Eve with the notion of "playing god" (Gen. 3:1-5). It amazes me that the temptation to make ourselves as gods was around even in the beginning. This was not a design of God, but a result of our own evil intentions that we wrestle with when exercising free will. Listening to the serpent's temptation, Eve began to observe the tree of forbidden fruit and realized how delicious it appeared. Her fixation on the forbidden fruit and having the understanding of God becomes the catalyst of poor choices. She was not content in how God had created her; instead, she desired to have that which was not intended for her. The apostle James illustrates this sequence of events in his writing. James writes, "Let no one say when he is tempted, 'I am being tempted by God,' for God cannot be tempted with evil, and he himself tempts no one. But each person is tempted when he is lured and enticed by his own desire. Then desire when it has conceived gives birth to sin, and sin when it is fully grown brings forth death" (Jas. 1:13-15).

DECEPTION AND MANIPULATION

Deception is a tool often used by others in order to obtain something they desire. The tactic of deceiving by manipulating common knowledge often leads innocent people into trouble as a result of their trust in those who are speaking with them. When words and meanings are being twisted, the manipulator can appear to be wise and harmless while the reality is he is a wolf in sheepskin. This is the situation Eve finds herself in when conversing with the serpent.

Every trickster understands the secrets to the trade of deception. As a lion studies its prey before making its move, the serpent has studied Eve and learned her desires so that he might use them to entice her to betray God (1 Pet. 5:8). Through half-truths the serpent beguiles Eve, not with fruit, but with the chance to be like God. In John 8:44, Jesus gave a good description of the serpent, Satan, when likening some of the corrupt religious leaders to him. Jesus said, "He was a murderer from the beginning, and does not stand in the truth, because there is no truth in him." Not only does Jesus say there is no truth in the devil, he drives home just how heinous his lies are in the rest of the verse, "When he lies, he speaks out of his own character, for he is a liar and the father of lies."

Notice the tricks of the serpent. The serpent begins by pretending he could not believe God would actually give such a commandment about not eating of the fruit, as if it were preposterous. Once the woman confirmed it, the serpent sowed doubt in her mind. Rather than completely undermining God's word, the serpent offers an alternative interpretation of God's reasoning. He begins to manipulate God's instruction. The serpent might as well have said, "God doesn't really mean that; God just doesn't want you to be like him. He doesn't want you to be wise and understanding like he is." I can imagine it is at this moment where he gently turns Eve's cheek to face her toward the tree. It is then that the fruit glistens as if the dew were still dancing in morning sunlight. Mesmerized by the beautiful fruit, Eve snatched one off the branch and ate it. Immediately she shared some with Adam, and they both lost the purity of their minds. The serpent was able to deceive the couple into betraying their loving, creative God.

THE CONSEQUENCE OF BETRAYAL

"And they heard the sound of the LORD God walking in the garden in the cool of the day" (Gen. 3:8). Wow! Can you imagine living in a time in which the God who masterfully created us walked among us? The Garden of Eden was not only for the enjoyment of creation, but also for the enjoyment of its creator. In the cool of the day, God was walking among his creation, no doubt taking pleasure in it. As God walked among the garden, he was looking for his masterpiece—Adam. Calling out, God sought out Adam who had taken cover in order to hide his nakedness. What do you do when God is walking around calling for you? Do you run? Do you ignore it and hope God goes back home? Adam decided the best option would be to tell God where he was and explain himself. During Adam's discussion with God, the truth is uncovered, and God finds out they have eaten of the forbidden fruit. When confronted about their disobedience, Adam points his finger at Eve who points her finger at the serpent. Nobody wants to take the blame! "It's not my fault, blame them" was the response Adam and Eve had. How easy it is to put the blame on others for our mistakes? How often are we caught in disobedience and try to make it someone else's fault?

Adam and Eve had a choice to make. Will they listen to God or to others? Do they make the rules, or do they allow God to make them? Whose voice will they listen too? When confronted with an opportunity to obey God and trust his direction, they chose poorly. Adam and Eve chose themselves over God. This decision impacts everything and everyone around them. Their selfish desire to be like God leads to significant consequences. Childbearing will become more painful for Eve and providing for the family will become more difficult for Adam. God had earlier warned Adam and Eve about the consequences of poor choices.

Each of us is faced with the same choice that Adam and Eve faced. No, it's not a fruit tree; it is the choice of who we will allow to rule in our lives. Will we rule our own lives or allow God to? Will we betray the trust of God, or will we validate it? We can choose God or ourselves, right or wrong, truth or falsehood, clarity or deception. We have a choice, and every morning when we get out of our bed and make that choice, we should remember that betraying God comes with eternal consequences. These consequences will be discussed in a later chapter; for now, it is enough to remember that the betrayal of God by Adam and Eve began in their hearts' desire for that which was not meant for them.

As Joshua neared the end of the conquest of Canaan (the land God had given to Israel) and neared the time of his death, he admonished the nation to "Choose this day whom you will serve…But as for me and my house, we will serve the LORD" (Josh. 24:15). Just as Adam and Eve were offered the choice of serving God or themselves and just as Israel was offered the choice, we are also given the same choice. To choose God means that we will listen to him, obey him, commit completely to him, and allow him to rule every facet of our lives. To pursue God is to acknowledge our betrayal and begin to walk with him as we implement his teachings. Sin entered into the world because God's masterpiece, humanity, has chosen poorly and has betrayed the creator.

THE CHOICE OF BETRAYAL

In his creative process, God did not create sin. According to the book of Mark, sin is created by what is inside of us (Mark 7:14-19). The freedom to choose will always offer the opportunity to abandon God for sin; however, it also offers the opportunity to make good choices. Sin, the betrayal of God, is what defiles a person who was created good. "For from within, out of the heart of man, come evil thoughts, sexual immorality, theft, murder, adultery, coveting, wickedness, deceit, sensuality, envy, slander, pride, foolishness" (Mark 7:21-22). While this list is not exhaustive, it serves as an example of poor choices that betray God and his purpose for our lives.

A study in the poor choices of Adam and Eve will reveal several lessons to us. The desires in our hearts can entice us to disobey and betray our God who lovingly created us. Just as the financial desires of the apostle Judas led him to give Jesus over to murderers (Matt. 26:47-50), our own desires can lead to betrayal and separation from God. The temptation to blame others when our betrayal is caught must be overcome as we strive to take responsibility for our choices. As sin forever changed the course of life for Adam, Eve, and humanity, it continues to change our lives, this world we live in, and our relationships if it is not dealt with. A creative and loving God created and chose humanity to be called his own, only to be rejected for our own desires and pursuits.

SUMMARY

- You were created very good.
- God loves you enough to let you choose.
- Humanity betrayed God in sin.

QUESTIONS

1. What does this story illustrate about humanity?
2. How does humanity's sin impact its innocence?
3. How does the sin of humanity impact its relationship with God?
4. Why do you think Adam and Eve betrayed God?
5. What are ways you have betrayed God in your life?

CHAPTER FOUR

THE FRUSTRATED GOD

GENESIS 6:5-8
GALATIANS 5:19-21

Chances are you have felt your fair share of frustration, whether at school, work, home, or really anywhere at all. It may be that you were frustrated when that coworker received the promotion you deserved. Maybe you feel frustrated with your spouse who just cannot seem to put away the dishes or properly install the roll of toilet paper. Maybe it is frustration at your child for not listening or your parents for always asking when they will have a grandchild. It does not matter what stage of life you are in, there will always be periods of frustration.

God is not immune to frustration. In fact, by the time we reach Genesis 6, we find the world has become so corrupt that God is beyond frustrated. Many years have passed since the betrayal of Adam and Eve. The earth is now heavily populated with mankind and new acts of betrayal are being invented every day. In fact, Scripture says, "The LORD saw that the wickedness of man was great in the earth, and that every intention of the thoughts of his heart was only evil continually" (Gen. 6:5). Earth became so ungodly and corrupt that the next several chapters of Genesis describe God's renewal of creation and starting over again with the family of Noah!

WHY WAS GOD FRUSTRATED?

Think of a person, walking on a dark night, who gets splashed by a passing taxi. With the help of a distant light, he notices he is now muddy and brushes the spot off the best he can and continues his walk. Growing closer to the light, he sees that the muddy spot is worse than he first realized. Standing under the light, the man notices there is actually very little white left on his white shirt and that he must now change clothing.

The closer God looked at creation, the more he saw arrogance and wickedness abounding. He had designed creation for many things, but wickedness and betrayal was certainly not one of them. It seems that like the man who realized his filthiness in the light decided a change must take place, God shined light on creation and concluded the same. A God who loved what he had created and declared good was heartbroken at the betrayal which took place. The longer the betrayal went on, the more frustrated God became. Just as humanity had help in the initial betrayal by Adam and Eve, humanity once again defied God by succumbing to fleshly desires.

This is a common theme with the people of God. Throughout the Old Testament, God's people continually caused frustration as they sought their own wicked desires rather than those of their loving creator. In the book of Exodus, the Jewish nation was enslaved by an Egyptian Pharaoh who began treating them poorly. Moses, a Jew who was saved at birth by Pharaoh's daughter and grew up in the imperial house, would eventually lead the Jews to rebel against the Egyptian ruler and take them to a new land. In Exodus, the initial excitement of the newly freed Jews would soon be replaced with longing the abundance of Egypt, even though that abundance was accompanied by slavery. Their thanksgiving turned into grumbling and their praise of God returned to the idols of Egypt. The wickedness of this generation began to build a divide between them and God. It began to grieve their Savior as we saw much earlier in Genesis 6.

THE GRIEF OF GOD

What does it mean to grieve the heart of God? Did you know that was possible? In Genesis 6:6 it says that God not only regretted making humanity, but it also "grieved him to his heart." What a powerful statement! A good creator who dearly loved creation has been so hurt he now grieves. Humanity has betrayed him so much that God begins to regret the decision of breathing life into his most prized possession. Does this mean he has stopped loving humanity? By no means! Humanity has deeply disappointed God in betrayal by not living as we were designed to live. We were living against the very nature God instilled in us.

A friend who betrays us brings grief and regret to our hearts. It is not that we don't love the friend; rather, it is because of our love that we grieve. A mother's heart is broken when her child makes poor choices that will impact his or her life forever. Think of a child who has broken the laws of the land and must face legal punishment. Parents desire their children to be productive, successful members of society and are grieved by the imprisonment of that child. Why are they grieved? The child has betrayed his parents, his upbringing, and the very purpose that was instilled in him. It is not that love was lost for the incarcerated child; it is the sense of betrayed values and the grief of loss that hurts the parents.

It is the same with God. God designed humanity with the purpose to love him and tend to creation (Gen. 1-2). His plan was quickly derailed, and by Genesis 6, something has gone very wrong—humanity has turned its back on God and chosen to betray him in sin. The regret of God is not the removal of love, but a change in course. It is important to understand that although God is frustrated with creation, his actions are not intended for evil, but for purification and of giving creation a second chance. Out of frustration, God was ready to wipe the slate completely clean, but a man named Noah caught his attention. Noah sought after God, and his family would become the Adam and Eve of his day by repopulating the earth and following after God. Rather than destroying everything, God decides to recreate the world and populate it anew, beginning with Noah's family by means of a great flood (Gen. 6:9-9:18). In order to understand what brought humanity to the point of bringing such frustration to its Creator, we must understand the origin of sin.

THE INTENTIONS OF HUMAN HEARTS

The origin of sin within an individual is summarized by Genesis 6:5 as the setting of one's thoughts on evil intentions. These thoughts ultimately lead to the act of betrayal and the frustration of God. Jesus deals with this same concept in Mark 7:14-23. Here, Jesus teaches what occurs when sinfulness and betrayal happen to us—they are an external source that contaminate the internal spirit. Jesus affirms this in his instruction, "What comes out of a person is what defiles him. For from within, out of the heart of man, come evil thoughts, sexual immorality, theft..." (Mark 7:20-23).

It is often believed that behavior drives one's thoughts. The truth of the matter is that more often than not, our behavior is directed by the inner thoughts of our hearts. As we will elaborate on in the next section, James 1:14-15 illustrates that sin begins within and then drives action. The implication of this is that God is not only frustrated by what creation is doing, but he is even frustrated by how it is thinking. God is frustrated by the sins of the heart above everything else.

MODERN-DAY FRUSTRATIONS

God's frustration led to a new beginning in the days of Noah. As you read and learn the Bible, it will become clear that humanity did not learn its lesson. In fact, it was not long after the flood that humanity repopulated and began to frustrate God in betrayal and sin. This led to God choosing a people for himself called Israel who would become an example to others. Likewise, Israel started the same way we have seen time and time before. In the beginning, they fell head over heels in love with the creator, but they soon began to choose their own desires over those of the God who deeply loved them. A reading of the Old Testament will show God's frustration with Israel's pattern of betrayal and his discipline. Israel follows God before eventually choosing their own desires. Seeing their poor choices, God gives multiple warnings and sends them into time out—a time of exile in other nations. Once they apologized, changed their ways, asked for forgiveness, and again pursued God, they were allowed home again, only to make the same mistakes years later. This is the saga of God's chosen people. It is a story of joy and heartbreak that reveals a cyclical pattern that continued into the time of Christ and even into today.

Humanity has not changed much. Sin is still a constant struggle and must be dealt with. The key to dealing with any problem is being able to identify it. God becomes frustrated at the desires of our hearts that are not intended for us. How do we know what these are? The good news is that in the Bible we can find several examples of sinful intentions. While not exhaustive, some of the desires that are not designed for God's creation can be found in Mark 7:14-23 and Galatians 5:19-21. These markers of unhealthy desires and actions begin to paint a picture of just how far humanity has strayed from its creator. When compared to the creation account in Genesis, innocence has been cast off in exchange for immorality.

SUMMARY

- You were created very good.
- God loves you enough to let you choose.
- Humanity betrayed God in sin.
- Betrayal frustrated and grieved God.

QUESTIONS

1. How do we frustrate God today?

2. How does the grief of God illustrate his desires, dreams, and plans for humanity?

3. We all struggle with sin, what are some things we can do to overcome that struggle?

4. Why do you think God continues to try and make things work with humanity?

CHAPTER FIVE

THE SEPARATED GOD

ISAIAH 59:1-2
ROMANS 7:13-25

Choices are a wonderful part of life, until you (or others) have to bear the consequences of a poor one. Within only a week of my daughter's birth, we made a trip to the emergency room due to the health issues my wife was having. What we thought would be a quick trip for us turned into a long night lasting into the wee hours of the morning. After sitting in the ER several hours, our luck with my daughter's temperament was about to change. Waking in a panic, my daughter began to cry inconsolably. After considering our options, we decided on a diaper change. Because mommy was not feeling well, it was up to dad. No problem! I had been doing this for a week and even had experience doing it as a Certified Nurse Assistant. Pulling out the diaper, I quickly moved into position. Having removed the dirty diaper, I proceeded to place the clean one under her. In that moment, my night would take a drastic change of course, and I would be famously known by the staff in the ER for eternity. Before I could get the new diaper clasped, my daughter took aim and fired. Moments later I was in a desperate need of a shower and change of clothes. Now, many of you have children and grand-children, and we all realize that this happens. However, we were in the ER, over thirty minutes from our home, and I had no change of clothes with me. Just imagine what I looked and smelled like the rest of the night as we anxiously awaited to be discharged. Imagine the embarrassment I felt as the nurses looked, snickered, and closed the curtain only to open it again with three or four other nurses who then proceeded to giggle. And why did this happen? Why was I counting down the seconds until I could shower off the filth and smell? It was my consequence for a really bad decision.

This is a picture of how God views the sinfulness in our lives. As God looks at his wonderful creation, he desperately wants to love on us and spend time with us, but something must be accomplished. The filth in our lives must be cleaned, and the stench of sin must be removed. The filth that kept others from me illustrates the barrier separating God and his creation.

SIN SEPARATES US FROM GOD

Isaiah 59:1-2 teaches a vital lesson for humanity concerning its relationship with the creator. It reads, "Behold, the LORD's hand is not shortened, that it cannot save, or his ear dull, that it cannot hear; but your iniquities have made a separation between you and your God, and your sins have hidden his face from you so that he does not hear." The choices we make have a great impact on the outcome of our physical and spiritual lives. Our choices can bring us closer to God or they can create distance and separation from God. The creator does not desire to be distanced from his most loved creation, but a perfect God can have no interaction with sin, and sin must therefore be dealt with before we can encounter the composer of creation.

The passage begins by identifying that the problem does not lie with God. It is not that he is too far away from us or that he is outside of earshot and cannot hear our requests and needs; rather, his arms are long enough, and he is able to listen to our prayers. The real issue is a barrier that separates us. It is a barrier that God desperately desires to cross but must be removed in a joint effort between you and him. The wall of separation is representative of our sin.

Our sins create a separation between God and his creation. Sin creeps in and builds a wall when we do not pay attention. This wall goes unnoticed until we need God but find ourselves separated from the one who desperately desires to help us. How is this wall built? If you continue reading in this chapter of Isaiah, the wall is built by defiled hands and a lying, wicked tongue (Isa. 59:3). In a nut shell, the wall is built from various evil activities, desires, and words (Isa. 59:3-21).

THE CONFUSION OF SIN

Robert Cox uses a wonderful illustration of the impact of sin in our lives and how it separates us from God. Using Romans 7:13-25, he illustrates the problems that sin will cause in our lives. These issues were experienced by the apostle Paul over 2,000 years ago! If Paul experienced these difficulties because of sin, it stands to reason we likely experience similar struggles. This passage teaches five ways that sin impacts our lives: enslavement, confusion, theft of confidence, condemnation, and options. Let's briefly look at these five items in a bit more detail.

First, sin enslaves me (Rom. 7:14). As a debtor is enslaved to her creditor, those who live in sin are enslaved to it. Consider addiction. Many addicts find themselves unable to cease feeding their habit. What began as curiosity soon turned to a craving and eventually an addiction. Addicts go into chemical withdrawal when attempting to wean off the drug of choice. Their body sends signals to the brain telling the brain they cannot survive without the drug because the chemical has become the master of the body. The addict lacks control of his or her own life and lives to serve the growing addiction. This is a negative cycle that often leads to destruction of the addict and those he or she loves the most. In the same way, sin owns our lives until we allow the creator to set us free from our dependency on it.

Second, sin confuses me (Rom. 7:15). Here, the apostle Paul struggles with sinfulness and an understanding of some of the desires he has given into. There are people who live so deeply in sin that they no longer know what is right and wrong. The good guy becomes the villain, and the victim becomes the oppressor. The result of sin leads to confusion in humans. It often blurs the lines between right and wrong.

Third, sin steals my confidence (Rom. 7:18-19). Paul illustrates not only the confusion of what is right and wrong, but also the lack of confidence that confusion causes. An individual struggling with sin may feel there is no way out, so he thinks he might as well give into the behavior, thought, or lifestyle. Many of us know the right thing to do but find ourselves lacking the confidence to do it. Sin, although it seems fun at times, can steal our confidence that things can be better and that there is a God who deeply loves and desires to help us.

Fourth, sin condemns me (Rom. 7:23-24). "Who will deliver me from this body of death?" The apostle understood the life of sin leads to condemnation. This concept is not popular today. We don't like being told something is wrong. The world we live in admittedly protests the idea that a loving, creative God could send someone to Hell for his or her mistakes. The reality, however, is that God does not condemn humanity; each individual condemns himself by his poor choices that go against God. In fact, Hell and condemnation were intended for Satan and his demons, not for humanity (Matt. 25:41).

Finally, sin calls me to make a choice (Rom. 7:25). By the end of the passage, Paul acknowledges that with his mind he serves God and with his flesh he serves sin. He understands there is an internal battle raging. This battle will eventually culminate in requiring a choice. Scripture teaches that we cannot serve two masters (Matt. 6:24). Just as we cannot serve both God and money, we cannot serve both good and evil. A choice must be made between godliness and worldliness. Just as every addict eventually hits a point of decision (often called "rock bottom"), we will eventually be required to choose a side: God's or Satan's. God will not make that choice for you; it is yours and yours alone. But what informs our choice?

THE CHOICE OF GOOD AND EVIL

A consideration of what drives our choice to sin is best began in the book of James. The brother of Jesus writes a letter to persecuted Christians that provides hope and comfort in the midst of suffering. It is within this text that we can also see insight concerning sinfulness. Before we move on to the text, I want you to do a brief exercise. Take out a sheet of paper and list three sins. Once those have been listed, beside each one, write what thoughts and considerations went into making that decision. Chances are, if you do this enough, you will see a pattern develop that begins with selfishness.

James 1:12-15 teaches those who pursue God that he may allow them to be tempted, but God, himself, does not actually present the temptation. This is important because for God to taunt us with sin is to go outside of his perfect nature. Rather, James writes, "each person is tempted when he is lured and enticed by his own desire." Aha! It is not the devil who made me do it; it is my own personal desire. To make certain the reader understands the germination of sin, James explains, "Then desire when it has conceived gives birth to sin, and sin when it is fully grown brings forth death." Once again, God does not send us to the dwelling created for Satan and his demons; it is a choice each individual makes on his or her own. We must choose death or life. God offers the choice of life. If one does not accept this choice, it is not the fault of God, but the foolishness of the individual. How do we choose life? It begins with dealing radically with that which separates us from our creator—sin.

DEALING RADICALLY WITH SIN

I have struggled to understand why humanity, including myself, would be willing to go to extremes to rid themselves of cancerous cells in the body by flooding themselves with poison while paying little attention to the cancerous sin that carries eternal consequences. In Matthew 5:27-30, Jesus uses imagery to illustrate the severity of sin and the radical nature in which we are to rid our lives of it. For example, he teaches that those who sin by the hand are called to cut it off. There is no evidence of the early church literally tearing out their eye or cutting off their hand because of sin. Rather, Jesus is exposing the severity of the problem and the extreme treatment that is needed to rectify it. It is counterintuitive to deal radically with a disease that will destroy our physical body while neglecting to deal with the disease that will destroy our spiritual one. God loves you and desperately wants you to come to him, but the sin that separates you from him must be dealt with radically. God desires his prized creation to rid themselves of those things that are not in his own character so that we can be reunited with him and receive blessings, inheritance, and adoption. Sin separates us from God, but God never gives up in his pursuit of reconciliation.

SUMMARY

- You were created very good.

- God loves you enough to let you choose.

- Humanity betrayed God in sin.

- Betrayal frustrated and grieved God.

- Sin separates us from God and must be dealt with.

QUESTIONS

1. How do the topics in this section relate to the story of Adam and Eve?

2. How does this information relate to the overall story being told?

3. What are radical ways of dealing with sin in your life? Why do we often struggle to be radical in this?

4. Thinking back to the previous lesson, what does this say about the passage in Galatians 5:19-21?

CHAPTER SIX

THE LONGING GOD

JEREMIAH 29:11-14
ACTS 17:26-27

When you pursue something, how do you go about it? In college, I first saw my wife from across the choir hall. She was beautiful, and I longed to meet her. Over time, we began to talk, then sit together, and eventually date each other. I went out of my way to ensure she was happy and did everything possible to secure my place in her life. Silly things like Valentine's Day and anniversaries were taken more seriously and attention to detail became a specialty of mine. The goal was to pursue and marry her. As I anticipated the end result, each step I took was focused and thoughtful.

For many, the idea of God creates an image of a larger than life figure who looks down on his creation as pawns in a game of toil and misery. This concept creates the picture of a being that cares neither for the desires nor the affection of its creation. It is a grim, self-centered, dejecting portrait. However, as we examine the ancient Scriptures given to us by God, we find that he longs for creation to be reconciled with him. The view of a self-serving God has more in common with Roman mythology and the games played by its gods than the love and pursuit found in the reality of the God of the Bible. The creator longs for his creation to have a life that is full of purpose and love (John 10:10). This concept is found throughout the Old and New Testaments. One place of particular significance is found in the words of the prophet Jeremiah.

GOD'S DESIRE FOR YOU

Fathers of teenage daughters can often be heard asking the new boyfriend "What are your intentions with my daughter?" The aim is to find out exactly what the young boy desires and where his heart lies. The answer can have a profound impact on the future of the young man in more ways than one. Similarly, we often struggle with the intentions of God. We may know that he is present and even that he is all powerful and knowing, but we may still struggle to find the answer to the question posed to the young boy. However, there is good news! God has not only provided us with his intentions, he has also made certain they were recorded and passed on for thousands of years so that we could know exactly what he wants for us.

The prophet Jeremiah spoke to a people who had left God and struggled to return to him. God's people were experiencing all kinds of hardship because of their refusal to follow the creator. They had ignored the teachings of God and were now reaping the consequences. It may seem harsh to some that God would allow his chosen people to be taken away to other lands, but it is a form of discipline in order to correct the behavior. As parents discipline their children to correct a poor attitude or behavior, God reproves Israel out of his love in hopes they would realize their wrong and return to him. In fact, God sent prophets to repeatedly warn his children of this consequence, but the people paid no attention. In the midst of Israel's disobedience, God did not give up on them. God pursued Israel even as they ran from his embrace. Why? The love of God is great and longs for reconciliation with his masterpiece.

We often have a struggle similar to those in the Old Testament. There are times in each of our lives where we question the love of God and his intentions for us. In Jeremiah 29:11-14 we see God's reassurance for his original plan laid out by the prophet. Let's read this verse together: "For I know the plans I have for you, declares the LORD, plans for welfare and not for evil, to give you a future and a hope. Then you will call upon me and come and pray to me, and I will hear you. You will seek me and find me, when you seek me with all your heart. I will be found by you, declares the LORD, and I will restore your fortunes and gather you from all the nations and all the places where I have driven you, declares the LORD, and I will bring you back to the place from which I sent you into exile" (Jer. 29:11-14).

Jeremiah declares that God has a plan for our future. Contrary to the belief of some, God's plan includes wholeness, purpose, and hope. His plan includes being found and overcoming the barrier sin creates between him and his creation. The idea that God is "out to get us" is ludicrous. He is desperate to reunite with us and willing to do whatever it takes to make that happen. God's plan for creation is one of blessing, not curse. Ancient Israel failed miserably and chose to walk away from their protector. Even in the midst of their disobedience and rejection, God reminds them of his intention for their lives. This reminds me of the story of the son who took his inheritance and wasted it away to the point of poverty. He returned home, expecting to be treated as a servant of the house, but his father ran to him, placed the royal robes upon him, and restored him as his son, not a servant (Luke 15:11-32). The father did not desire to curse his son, but to restore and bless him. God views us the same way. Our creator offers promises, but they come with conditions. God's promises are freely given while being conditional in nature.

PROMISES AND CONDITIONS

Throughout the Bible, the promises of God have always been conditional. For example, when Joshua takes leadership of Israel after the death of Moses, God promises to be with him as long as he follows the laws and intentions of God (Josh. 1:1-9). God tells Joshua that the promise of success and retention of the Promised Land, Canaan, would come to fruition only if he continued to follow God and listen to his teachings. The promise was success in the mission of God. The condition involved obedience and teachability. In a similar way, Jeremiah reminds the people of Israel many years later that God intends for them to possess the land he had promised them, but retention of that land is conditional.

Jeremiah 29:12-14 offers three promises to the dispersed people of God. *First, God offers the promise of listening to them.* Remember the passage in Isaiah that teaches God is able to hear us once our sins have been removed (Isa. 59:1-2)? Likewise, God is able to listen to the cries of his people as they long to return to the promises of God. The God of Israel wants to help his creation and reunite with them. He does not desire to leave them exiled from the promised land of Canaan.

Second, God promises that they will be able to find him. Jeremiah records God as saying "You will seek me and find me…" (29:13). This is important. Imagine being exiled for many years and generations, wondering where God is and not knowing how to find him. Jesus drives this promise home in Mathew 7:7-8. God promises his availability to Israel, but he doesn't stop there.

The third promise God makes is that of salvation. God states that he will rescue Israel from exile! These people have been scattered around the known world away from the land God had given them. In this third promise, God reminds them that not only is he making himself available to hear their longings and to be found by those who look for him, but he is also guaranteeing the deliverance of his children.

These promises come with a conditional statement that seems easy at first but later reveals its difficult nature. Jeremiah records that these promises will be fulfilled "when you seek [God] with all your heart" (29:13). There you have it. Israel, as well as contemporary readers, must seek God with all of their heart in order to find him and receive his promises. These are not promises of material wealth and health; they are promises of something much deeper; promises that can only be experienced as we pursue the God who pursues us. How does one pursue God? How do we seek our creator with all of our heart? Great questions!

PURSUING THE CREATOR

In Acts 8: 26-40 we read a story that gives insight on what it means to seek after God with all of one's heart. It is the story of a man, an Ethiopian eunuch, who loved God so much that he traveled a journey of about six months in order to stand outside of the Jewish temple and worship God. This individual would not have been able to enter into the gathering of God's people to worship according to Jewish law (Deut. 23:1) but still desired to journey from Ethiopia to Jerusalem so that he could stand on the peripherals and come close to God. Little did he know how close God actually was. An estimate of one thousand miles traveled over about six months just to view the worship of God—that is dedication! This individual sacrificed time and money in order to seek out God. As a groom seeks his bride, the eunuch sought God with time and finances.

The trip to Jerusalem was only the beginning of the eunuch's search for God. Acts 8:28 reminds us that this man was a student of the writings of God. As he traveled on the road, the eunuch was reading from Isaiah the prophet and seeking to understand his message. To seek God with all of our heart requires not only sacrifice of time and money, but also a thirst for the wisdom and knowledge of God. That thirst is quenched in the study and exploration of the Bible. Often we struggle with studying God's Bible because we encounter hard concepts, and we need some help. This is a great opportunity to continue the pursuit of God by asking those who have gone before us for help. The Ethiopian asked Philip for help in Acts 8:31-34. This request opened a wide door of understanding that provided the eunuch with information, understanding, and direction. It is never too late to ask for help. Asking for assistance can open doors that we may have never noticed before.

The pursuit, or seeking of God with all of our heart, does not end with knowledge. We must put into practice the teachings we hear. Notice that Philip started with the passage from Isaiah 53 and began to share "the good news about Jesus." This good news led to an understanding of God's promises, and to the conditions of that promise. As they were riding down the road, it appears the Ethiopian had been told about the necessity of baptism and how it brings forgiveness and the Spirit of God (Acts 2:38, Matt. 18:19-28). This new information led the eunuch to quickly act on God's request. Notice that he does not procrastinate once he is made aware of the necessary action to be taken. In fact, the eunuch notices water and demands to be immersed in it (Acts 8:37). Pursuing God with all of our heart includes immediate action on what is found concerning God's instructions. What are you willing to do in order to pursue God with all of your heart? Like a horse with blinders to focus him on the task, what blinders do you need in your life to help you focus on pursuing the creator who longs for you?

SUMMARY

- You were created very good.
- God loves you enough to let you choose.
- Humanity betrayed God in sin.
- Betrayal frustrated and grieved God.
- Sin separates us from God and must be dealt with.
- God longs for our reconciliation.

QUESTIONS

1. What does God want for your future?
2. What are signs that a person is pursuing something with "all of his or her heart?"
3. What does Jeremiah 29:11-14 teach us about God's love for us?
4. How do we know the Ethiopian was pursuing God?
5. How did the Ethiopian respond to God's desire for him and why is he a good illustration of Jeremiah 29:11-14?

CHAPTER SEVEN

THE PURSUING GOD

LUKE 2:1-21
MARK 1:1-11

What lengths would you go to for those you love? When someone wrongs you and turns her back on you, do you require her to approach you or are you willing to go to her in order to be reconciled? The God who longs for us to pursue him does not hesitate to begin his pursuit of humanity. God desperately desires to see his masterpiece saved and cherished. This desire led to the most significant event in all of history, his return to earth.

The Jews longed for God's rule on the earth. The common belief in the first century was that God's return would be like a king who returns victorious from battle. Little did they know their expectations would be shattered as God chose to come in human form, as the child of a simple virgin rather than as a God ready to conquer Rome. There was nothing glamorous about the birth of God in the flesh.

Luke 2:1-21 follows the announcement to the parents of Jesus and John the Baptizer concerning the coming Savior. It is in this chapter that we see God come to creation as each one of his created beings has, in the form of a smiling, giggling, crying baby. During the days of Caesar Augustus, the savior was born in the town of Bethlehem. At the birth of Jesus, angels chose to visit some shepherds who seem to have been waiting for a savior. The angel began by proclaiming to them, "Fear not, for behold, I bring you good news of great joy that will be for all the people" (Luke 2:10). Notice the encouragement offered by the angels. Not only were they bringing good news to the shepherds, it was good news for all people that they brought! That's right! It's good news for you and me as well. At this announcement, a group of angels appeared and began singing about the amazing God as the shepherds quickly ran to find the child. God did not end his story by asking us to pursue him; he began to pursue us.

GOD PURSUES HIS MASTERPIECE

While God longs for humanity to return to him, there is an almost unexpected turn of events in Scripture. God calls us to pursue him with all of our heart, but the creator also pursues us! As you run closer to God, he runs towards you, his masterpiece. The clearest evidence of this is the arrival of God on the earth in human form.

The New Testament begins with an introduction to a new prophet, John. John the Baptizer arrives on scene after nearly four hundred years of silence from God. The world in which John lived was controlled by the Roman Empire. This empire had conquered most of the ancient world and now found itself riddled with internal and external tensions. It was a time of fear, uprisings, and rebellion. This sets the stage for the prophet John who prepares the world for Jesus Christ, God in flesh. It is on this stage where God will make the ultimate, all-in attempt to pursue his work of art that he so deeply loves.

Mark 1:1-8 introduces us to the man John the Baptizer. This passage indicates that John was a prophet who not only sounded the part, but looked similar to other well known Old Testament prophets in both lifestyle and action (see 2 Kings 1:8 and Zech. 13:4). The message of John is found in Mark 1:7-8, "After me comes he who is mightier than I...he will baptize you with the Holy Spirit." This cousin of Jesus came to turn the world's attention back to its artist. The God who seemed so distant was on his way and desired that all would confess their sins and follow him. It was as John the Baptizer spoke that Jesus, the son of God, arrived. Jesus was around the age of thirty at this point.

GOD LIVES AS FLESH

Nobody wants to follow a leader who commands, "Do as I say, not as I do." Luckily, God's motto is, "Do as I do." In Mark 1:9-11, we see Jesus begin his ministry by being baptized by John. Going into the Jordan River, we see that Jesus is completely submerged in water because it says "he came up out of the water..." You must go down into the water in order to come out of it. As the Ethiopian eunuch would later be immersed in water, Jesus demonstrates how baptism takes place. Why? Because God desires to illustrate how to live in the flesh so that we can model our life after his. Immediately after Jesus is baptized, God confirms his decision and their relationship. The creator confirms that Jesus is God in the flesh, the Son of God. It is immediately after this that Jesus will face temptation while hungry and thirsty for forty days.

We find ourselves trying to live a life that pursues God, but the temptations can often seem overwhelming. We have a God who can sympathize with our temptations as one who was tempted himself. After Jesus' baptism, he is taken into the wilderness where Satan begins to tempt him. Satan tempts Jesus with the immediate satisfaction for his stomach by creating bread instead of relying on God. Jesus is then tempted with providing proof of who Jesus really says he is rather than allowing God to stand in his defense. Finally, Satan allures Jesus with an easy way out so that he does not have to suffer as a human by offering to relinquishing the earth to him (Matt. 4:1-11). At each temptation, Jesus recalls verses from the Old Testament to fend off Satan's attacks. As God walks in the flesh, he illustrates the ability to overcome temptation and sin when we rely upon the words and promises he has given.

Satan uses a variety of means to tempt us. We are tempted, as discussed previously, when our own desires get in the way of God's. I see many couples for counseling each week. Couples who seek help where infidelity is involved almost always struggle with blaming each other. One partner wants to blame the other and vice-versa. The reality is that both individuals almost always hold some of the blame. Often, the couple allowed Satan to secretly creep into their marriage and did not realize it until an affair had taken place. Why did an affair happen? While there are many possible answers, it almost always comes down to the adulterous party feeling his or her needs were not being met and his or her desires led to the arms of another lover to be fulfilled. While this is not an unforgivable sin, it illustrates that the lust and desires of our heart can lead us to sin in ways we never expected if we are not always on our guard. Most people do not wake up one day wanting to have an affair. In almost every case, Satan has laid a seed of desire that has been watered and cultivated.

This is how it is with temptation. Satan does not announce that he will begin tempting us; he spends time planning how to plant a seed of desire that he can slowly grow over time until it is in bloom. Once the time is right, Satan pounces on us with a temptation that can often seem overpowering. Jesus experienced this type of temptation. I'm certain Satan waited until Jesus was at his weakest point before offering the temptation to turn the stone into bread. But through reliance on God, Jesus was able to overcome.

GOD REVEALS THE SOLUTION

The solution to our sin problem lies in two places. It lies in our efforts to pursue God and in God's action as he pursues us. God understood the difficulty of following him, so he chose to pursue us in a way that allows him to identify with the temptations and trials we face on earth (Heb. 4:15). The solution is not only found in what we can do, though action and seeking is expected by God; it primarily lies in what God does at the cross. As we struggle with the sin barrier and breaking through it, take a lesson from Jesus and look first to God's book for the answers. The Bible will guide you closer to God and will help fend off the tempter. As the Ethiopian sought out God, you can pursue God as he pursues you.

SUMMARY

- You were created very good.

- God loves you enough to let you choose.

- Humanity betrayed God in sin.

- Betrayal frustrated and grieved God.

- Sin separates us from God and must be dealt with.

- God longs for our reconciliation.

- We pursue God as he pursues us.

QUESTIONS

1. Why do you believe God chose such a humble entrance into the world?

2. Why do you think Jesus was immersed in water? What was its significance?

3. When tempted to sin, what lessons can we take from Jesus in how to deal with it?

4. What temptations do you struggle with and what resources has God given to help you with them?

CHAPTER EIGHT

THE MERCIFUL GOD

LUKE 15:1-32
MATTHEW 18:10-14

What comes to mind when you hear the word mercy? For some of us, it is a wonderful word that is filled with love from God. For others, it is a reminder of the times as a child that our parents decided to "let it slide" rather than offer the punishment deserved. Couples may consider the mercy and grace they offer one another when they fall short of the perfect spouse. However you view it, the term creates a vivid picture filled with love and kindness.

Mercy and grace are often misunderstood today. The discussion of God's mercy and grace finds its way into heated discussions. Some believe these terms indicate that God extends forgiveness and a blind eye no matter the actions of the guilty party. Others believe mercy is to be extended but at a cost to the guilty party. The struggle to understand the mercy and grace of God is not new. In the New Testament, the apostle Paul frequented the subject in his teaching. Mercy and grace is not a "get out of jail free card," but it is also not earned. It is freely given and calls the recipient to a specific response.

PAUL AND MERCY

Paul discusses the merciful nature of God in his letter to the church located in Ephesus (located in what is now known as southern Turkey). In Ephesians 2:4-9 he illustrates the richness of mercy offered by God that is extended in love. Even at our lowest, most sinful point, God showed mercy and grace through the extension of a way out of sin through Jesus Christ. In fact, Ephesians 2:5 says that one has been saved by grace. Now, grace can save while still requiring action. I love the illustration of gifting a car. If a friend were to give you a fully paid for car, is the gift free or earned? No doubt we would agree that it was a free gift. Even though you have received a free gift, you do not have rightful ownership of that gift when you are handed the keys. Ownership is received when you drive to your local government office to get your name on the title, settle any taxes, receive plates and tags, and file the appropriate paperwork. After completing the tasks required by law, have you earned the car or was it a gift?

Before this passage, Paul had discussed the idea that we walked in evil ways before Christ came and God "stepped in." In the fourth verse, we see the same idea that is found in Romans 8 that explains how our sinful desires render us in need of a solution. This text shares the solution to this problem. Because we could not do it on our own, God helped us out and provided mercy.

THE MERCIFUL FATHER

The Bible records a story of a father who lost his son. As we saw previously, the son demanded his inheritance and squandered it away. Upon returning home, the father offered mercy to the son and accepted him back into the family. This story, found in Luke 15:1-32, is a picture of our relationship with God. Just as God always ran to meet those who returned to him wholeheartedly, his arms open wide to receive you and me when we pursue him. This text is important to revisit because it helps to clarify the definitions of mercy and grace.

First, it illustrates the point that mercy offers us a chance at forgiveness. It is through God's mercy that we have been saved and our sins can be dealt with. It was the love and mercy of God that drove him to pursue us. Throughout Paul's letters the mercy of God is illustrated. Jesus does the same many years earlier in the story of the runaway son. The father in the story was merciful to the son and forgave him of the debt that was owed. In the ancient culture, the decision of the younger brother would have been shameful to the family. The law of the land would have allowed the father to put out or even stone the son in order to return honor to his family. However, mercy was shown in the place of anger and judgment. The love of the father was able to cover and pardon the sins of the son. Likewise, God's love for us is filled with mercy and grace. God was merciful and provided a way for us to remove the barrier between him and his people. This was provided by the fleshly coming of God in Jesus Christ.

This mercy is not only forgiving but freely given. This second understanding of mercy brings hope to those who feel returning to God is impossible. We do not have to earn God's mercy; he loves us regardless of who we have been and what we have done. The prodigal son did not deserve the acceptance of his father and neither do we. We have repeatedly turned our back on God, but he still pursues us and desires to bless us.

Finally, this story illustrates the joy to be experienced in God's mercy. Do not forget about the older brother in the story. Hearing a ruckus at the house, the eldest brother returns to a joyful father who beams with light as he declares the return of his younger son. Rather than join the celebration, the faithful son chose to complain about the party and mercy shown to his brother. Of course, we never do this in our lives, do we? The Bible never tells us what became of the older brother. It leaves us to make the choice he was faced with. How do we react to the mercy of God in our lives and the lives of others?

THE JOY OF MERCY

One of my favorite passages that shares the pursuit, love, and mercy of God is found in Matthew 18:10-14. It is through this teaching that Jesus gives us a glimpse of the powerful mercy of God. We are faced with a creator who leaves the safety of the many in order to search out the one who is lost. God loves you so much that he desperately searches for you. Our creator is one who desires to extend mercy instead of punishment. While we must reap the consequences of our decisions, God desires to bless us and bring us back into his protection. As the father would not force the young son to return but eagerly waited for him, God will allow you to choose whether you accept his freely given mercy and grace. Through Jesus, God not only demonstrates his mercy, but freely offers it.

SUMMARY

- You were created very good.
- God loves you enough to let you choose.
- Humanity betrayed God in sin.
- Betrayal frustrated and grieved God.
- Sin separates us from God and must be dealt with.
- God longs for our reconciliation.
- We pursue God as he pursues us.
- Our creator is merciful and welcoming.

QUESTIONS

1. How does the story of the father and runaway son illustrate God's relationship with humanity?

2.   What example does the father set for us in the story?

3.   According to Jesus' teaching in Matthew 18:10-14, what is the will of God for his creation?

4.   Considering other lessons covered, what are some things God requires in order for us to receive his mercy and grace?

CHAPTER NINE

THE TEACHING GOD

LUKE 6:39-42; 9:23-26; 14:25-27

Children are beings who love to imitate others. This makes them entertaining to observe. A child will study the stride of his dad or the facial expressions of her mom and attempt to mimic them. Adult shoes left unattended find their way onto the feet of children as they pretend to be the owner of the shoes. The adult who is viewed by a child as special will become an instructor to them in the way of life. Like it or not, we all teach and are taught by others. Who we choose as our teacher will determine the success we achieve in our endeavor. It is the same principle that applies as we search out God. Who and what we choose to listen to will get us either closer or further from finding God.

Lonnie Davis, a wise minister once instructed, "Befriend those you want to be like. If you want to teach, surround yourself with great teachers. If you want to be successful, meet successful individuals who will act as a mentor, and if you want to be godly, submerge yourself in the lives of those who are dedicated to God." My friend's point was that the people we surround ourselves with become our instructors on how to live and succeed in life. This idea has been around for ages and is evident in the first century as God pursues his people. The life of Jesus was intended to not only allow God to empathize with his creation, but to demonstrate to mankind how we should live. Jesus lived as an example of what it means to live a life in pursuit of the pursuing God. He became our instructor. This instruction is not always easy to practice, but it completely satisfies.

A GOOD STUDENT

What makes someone a good student? Most universities have students from all walks of life and academic pursuits. In my time attending Harding University, I met studious learners who strived for perfection, as well as students who were happy to receive a passing grade as long as their social life was lively. As one who teaches, a different perspective of students has emerged. Good students become less about those with book smarts and more about those who can learn to apply the lesson.

As Jesus moves from the idea of loving your enemies to placing judgment on others, he plants a powerful understanding of what a good student is. Luke 6:39-42 indicates that a disciple is not one who is above his teacher, but like his teacher. The term disciple is indicative of one who learns from a master instructor. In the time of the New Testament, the Greco-Roman world was familiar with the term indicating a group of individuals who would follow their instructor (like Plato or Aristotle) around, listening and watching his every move. The goal of the disciple was to not only hear what was being taught, but to mimic his instructor in his own life. They are individuals who are serious students dedicated to practicing their instructor's lessons. Interestingly, the Bible teaches this same level of commitment as we pursue God. As students of God, we are called to be committed to his lifestyle.

TRAITS OF A FOLLOWER OF JESUS

One who follows Jesus as he or she seeks to find God carries various traits, two of which I wish to discuss here. First, the student will seek to understand the teachings of God. In Acts 17:11-12 we read the Bereans "were more noble than those in Thessalonica; they received the word with all eagerness, examining the Scriptures daily to see if these things were so. Many of them therefore believed, with not a few Greek women of high standing as well as men." Notice that even though the apostle Paul was teaching those who lived in Berea, they still checked it for accuracy by exploring the Word of God. As they searched what is known today as the Old Testament notice how eager they became. This text also identifies the second trait of a follower; prompt obedience.

As the Bereans checked for accuracy, we see that it lead to belief. Belief is more than simple acknowledgment. The Ethiopian helped us understand that belief includes action. Here, many who heard Paul speak identified the accuracy of the message and then acted upon it. There are many in the world who claim to have a message from God. Be on your guard and make sure the message and the directive come from the Bible. Take the attitude of those in Berea. Where does the Bible say one must only "ask Jesus into their heart" to be saved? Where does it say we can continue in a life of sin? What is the purpose of being immersed in water? Does the Bible actually say we can be forgiven of sins? We can only know the answers by examining these subjects and many other teachings in light of what the Bible actually says. It is for this reason that I always remind my congregation and students that I am imperfect. This imperfection means that they are to search for what I say in the Bible and believe it, not me. I am fallible; the Bible is not.

A FAITHFUL STUDENT

Most of us can think of a time when someone stopped being our friend when times became hard. These are fair weather friendships. Unfortunately, this is the type of relationship many have with God. It is easy to follow God when things seem to be going well, but when hardship comes and God seems a bit more distant, some run away from him rather than towards him. It is this subject that Jesus addresses with his followers as he explains the necessity of his death.

Luke 9:23-35 records a sober reminder of the serious nature of being a student of Jesus. Following Jesus will provide many wonderful experiences, but it will also have challenges and opposition. Look at the language he uses when speaking to his students about their pursuit. Jesus vividly illustrates the commitment involved in pursuing God. "If anyone would come after me, let him deny himself and take up his cross daily and follow me" (Luke 9:23). Did you catch that? Followers of Jesus are called to deny their worldly desires and place themselves on the cross. How does one crucify himself? Jesus teaches that it is not our own interests that matter as much as the interests of God. Like the son who threw away his inheritance, those who pursue God must realize desires like greed, lust, envy and self-gratification are not fulfilling. At the end of the day, those who pursue such things are left emptied and longing for home. Instead, we pursue God and become faithful students when we put those desires aside and place our journey toward God as our primary focus. Everything else can only distract from our goal.

The crucifixion of self is an important concept for the student. There are many times in life that we will be asked to deny what we want because it is not godly. We will be tempted to give in to ourselves and others even when we know it is bad for us and can separate us from God. This incredibly difficult task seems insurmountable in the moment, but by denying ourselves, we can take a step closer to God. Looking backward helps identify our weak points that we may need to be especially on guard for.

THE FOCUS OF A STUDENT

Luke 14:25-33 paints an interesting picture of what it means to follow Jesus and pursue God. Jesus is teaching the crowds that the pursuit of God is often difficult. God does not condone hatred of another person (1 John 2:11); therefore, the term hate is being used as an illustration, not a literal command. The concept here is a question of who is most important in the student's life. Jesus teaches that the pursuit of God comes before anything and anyone. The point is to help the student consider the cost of searching out God. This task is often costly in ways we have not considered. Those in the Middle East are often shunned from their families as they pursue God, and some countries will even persecute Christians—followers of Christ.

How does one renounce all she has? What does it mean? The idea Jesus is getting at in Luke 14:25-33 is, once again, an illustration directing the importance of our focus. A student who follows Christ toward God is to be focused solely on the task at hand. While God allows us to obtain homes, families, friends, jobs, and other things in life, he is very clear that these come secondary to the task at hand—pursuing him. The focus of a student is on his or her teacher. They put blinders on, so to speak, so that their vision is narrow and purposeful. These imaginary blinders allow us to not be distracted by deterrents as we journey toward God.

THE MISSION OF A STUDENT

The pursuit of our creator begins with learning how to live but also includes taking on the same mission of the teacher. Matthew 28:18-20 instructs that, as a student learns about following God, he or she is to instruct others in the way of God as well. Each one of us knows someone who has not chosen to follow God. They may be afraid of God. Some people are simply ill-informed about him or confused about his motives. Whatever the case is, God will place people in the lives of those who seek him that they can bring along in their journey. Those who pursue God will find others needing direction like the Ethiopian eunuch. He wants us to share the story of the God that loves his children so much that he would move heaven and earth to save them. God teaches you so that you can teach others.

SUMMARY

- You were created very good.
- God loves you enough to let you choose.

- Humanity betrayed God in sin.

- Betrayal frustrated and grieved God.

- Sin separates us from God and must be dealt with.

- God longs for our reconciliation.

- We pursue God as he pursues us.

- Our creator is merciful and welcoming.

- Jesus came to teach us to seek God.

QUESTIONS

1. What are characteristics of a good student?

2. What lessons can we learn from the Bereans?

3. How does one deny themselves? Why is this important to the pursuit of God?

4. What pulls our focus away from pursuing God?

CHAPTER TEN

THE CRUCIFIED GOD

ISAIAH 53
LUKE 23

God allowed his son, Jesus, to teach us how to follow him and how to deny ourselves in order to take on his mission. After about three years of ministry, around the age of thirty-three, Jesus was nearing the end of his life on earth. Jesus lived as a demonstration of God's mercy and pursuit as he taught others how to respond and begin their own pursuit of God. However, there is still the lingering problem of sin that must be dealt with. In an unexpected turn of events, the followers of Jesus will witness what had been prophesied hundreds of years ago in the book of Isaiah. It was from this text that the Ethiopian was reading when he invited Philip to help him understand the passage (Isa. 53:7-8; Acts 8:26-40).

THE PREDICTED SUFFERING OF GOD

God's prophet, Isaiah, declared that Jesus would come and be offered on a cross for our sins. He begins with an explanation of who Jesus would be. Isaiah 53:1-2 said Jesus "grew up...he had no form or majesty...and no beauty." Jesus was a regular person when he lived on earth. He was born as a baby, grew both physically and mentally, and was not the most popular kid at school. The pictures we often see of an athletic, good looking, and model-like Jesus is far from true. Jesus would have been an average, Jewish man who was not special because of how he looked, but for what he would do as God in flesh. In fact, Jesus was predicted to be despised and rejected by others. Isaiah 53:3 says he was "...a man of sorrows, and acquainted with grief...he was despised, and we esteemed him not." As God pursued humanity within his own creation, the prophet teaches that God would be rejected and eventually murdered on a cross. Isaiah indicated that God would come live among us, as one of us, in order to save us.

Why did Jesus suffer? What was the purpose of it? In humanity's rejection of Jesus, we rejected his father, God. This meant that a wall of separation was still in place between us and God. In order to deal with that separation, a price (or punishment) must be paid. In order to be a just God, there must be consequences. There cannot be justice without consequences for the guilty. Jesus offered himself as the one who would pay for the consequences of our sins throughout history. How could one man do that? If you put the eternal God on the cross, the payment is an eternal payment—it spans all of time. Isaiah 53:4-6 illustrates this. The passage indicates that this man whom Isaiah predicts will bear our sins. Did you notice that even though scripture foretells that Jesus will take on our sins, the prophet indicates that those who benefit from his death still think very little of him? Even though Jesus was looked down upon, the prophet teaches that he would take our place of suffering and punishment. It was punishment for self-ish-pursuits and turning away from God (Isa. 53:6).

Isaiah 53:7-9 paints a picture of how the Savior would suffer on our behalf. It says that he was oppressed and afflicted. Jesus would remain silent and not give a defense of himself when given the opportunity. The terminology used by Isaiah about the suffering of God is that of an innocent lamb that is led to be butchered. This dismal picture of the suffering of God would get even darker before the end. Not only would Jesus suffer at the hands of those he came to save, he would also become as sin before the eyes of God.

Jesus was not the only one who made a sacrifice. God was also willing to make the sacrifice for our benefit. Look again at Isaiah 53:10-12. How can God desire to "crush" this individual? I'm sure it was not easy for God to witness all that happened, but it was necessary if he was to be reunited with creation. An offering, sacrifice, and penalty had to be paid in order to remove the problem of sin and guilt. The cross was an expression of God's love for us (Rom. 5:8-9), and the way he chose to deal with our sin. In order for those who are imperfect to have a relationship with the perfect God, something perfect must be sacrificed. Jesus, the perfect God in flesh, was willing to die so forgiveness could be given.

THE FULFILLMENT OF GOD'S SUFFERING

The prophecy of Isaiah finds its fulfillment in the New Testament. Luke 23 shares the story of how God would fulfill the prophecy hundreds of years later. In the chapter before the crucifixion (Luke 22), Jesus began to explain to his disciples what was going to happen, and he was arrested shortly after. He is betrayed by one of his own followers, and then Peter denied knowing Jesus after his teacher's arrest. Luke 22:63-65 lets us know that Jesus was mocked and beaten prior to his trial. This was not allowed in Roman or Jewish law. An individual was to be brought before the council in trial before punishment was rendered. Additionally, the way they arrested Jesus was illegal, at best. It becomes clear to the reader of Luke 22 that the arrest and trial of Jesus would be vindictive rather than merited.

Chapter 23 of Luke shows Jesus being brought before Pilate, then taken to Caesar before the order to return him to Pilate. Luke 23:4 quotes Pilate as seeing no reason to punish Jesus. Pilate sees through the lies and half-truths of the accusers. Learning Jesus was from Galilee, he sent him to Herod who had jurisdiction for Galilean citizens. Herod was part Jewish, but neither Jew nor Roman liked him much. Herod was often motivated by fear in a time in which the Roman Empire was held together by a taut thread. After mocking and treating Jesus poorly, it was back to Pilate since Herod found no wrong in Jesus. At his return, Pilate suggested a punishment and then release. This did not go over well with the crowd.

Have you ever given way to a crowd of people even when you knew it was wrong? There are moments in each of our lives that we are faced with doing the right thing or the popular thing. Pilate was faced with this same decision, and his decision would forever change history. Pilate's decision determined a major turning point in the history of the world and fate of humanity.

Luke 23:18 records the volatile reaction of the crowd at Pilate's suggestion. In disagreement, the crowd demanded the most painful, humiliating death of the ancient world—crucifixion on a cross. This death was fitting only for the most violent offenders against Rome. It humiliated the individual and offered a slow, excruciating death as the criminal would gasp for air until his legs were broken so that he could no longer gather his breath. After begging the crowd to reconsider their demand, Pilate reluctantly granted their request and sent Jesus to be murdered.

THE CRUCIFIXION

Jesus had been tried, mocked, and whipped with cords containing glass, metal, and other objects meant to torture and tear the skin. After this, Jesus was required to carry the heavy cross-beam of the cross. This beam would slide onto the post that he would hang from. Take a moment and read Luke 23:26-49. Tried and crucified as a criminal, this perfect man still asked God to forgive those who tortured him as he agonized in torment on the cross (Luke 23:34).

The pain Jesus went through touched all three parts of an individual—physical, emotional, and spiritual. This pain is seen clearly in Matthew 27:22-50. Physically, Jesus was flogged thirty-nine times with a whip meant to torment and tear the skin. Many did not survive this beating. A crown was created out of large thorns and jammed onto his head and brow. As they stretched his arms across the rough cut cross-beam, they began to hammer a large nail into each wrist to ensure proper hanging. His feet were nailed to the cross as they placed him upright several feet above the ground for others to mock and spit at.

Emotionally, Jesus was humiliated as his clothes were stripped from him and soldiers mocked him. Insults, spit, and criticism were loosely thrown towards him. Imagine how vulnerable, how shameful it must have felt to be in this position. Knowing you did nothing wrong while being treated as an animal—friends and family deserted Jesus, and he was left on the cross with only his mother and one disciple to provide the presence of comfort.

Spiritually, Jesus took on the sins of the world. This means there was a spiritual issue at hand that God needed to deal with. As the "lamb led to slaughter," Jesus took on the sins of each one of us. He hung on the cross to pay a debt so that we would not be required to pay it. No matter how dark it looked, Jesus understood there was something much deeper going on. In his last moments, Jesus asked God to forgive those who had placed him on the cross. He asked the creator to use the crucifixion as the payment for our turning away from God. After a time on the cross, Jesus drew his last breath and surrendered his life. He no longer fought to stay alive; he gave himself to death.

WHY THE CRUCIFIXION?

Why did Jesus put himself through this? Why did God allow it to happen? Through it God has removed every obstruction between us and him. He pursued us to the point of death. It is through the suffering and death of Jesus that we are made pure, sinless, and holy by God. Through this atrocity we find beauty in forgiveness and sacrifice. Even though God did not want to see Jesus tortured in such a cruel way, we have been given the opportunity to seek him because of it.

SUMMARY

- You were created very good.

- God loves you enough to let you choose.
- Humanity betrayed God in sin.
- Betrayal frustrated and grieved God.
- Sin separates us from God and must be dealt with.
- God longs for our reconciliation.
- We pursue God as he pursues us.
- Our creator is merciful and welcoming.
- Jesus came to teach us to seek God.
- Jesus was tortured and murdered so we could find forgiveness.

QUESTIONS

1. How does the crucifixion demonstrate God's love for you and others?

2. What was the purpose of the torture and murder of Jesus?

3. Why did Jesus ask God to forgive those who put him on the cross?

4. How did you, personally, contribute to his placement on the cross?

5. How will you respond to the event of the cross?

CHAPTER ELEVEN

THE RESURRECTED GOD

LUKE 24
MATTHEW 28

Harding School of Theology has a tradition for their students who arrive on campus for week-long intensive courses. A meal is held for the students, and at the end of the meal, the students are asked to share their majors and projected date of completion. Going around the room asking for the graduation date of each individual was always an interesting experience. Many say they do not know when they will graduate and would often suggest they do not even see a glimmer of light at the end of their academic tunnel. After each student and faculty member was introduced, the academic advisor would stand up and speak to the students. His introduction went like this: "Hi, I am the academic advisor, and I am the light at the end of your tunnel." As the man who helped students figure out a plan for graduation, he allowed students to create a graduation plan and complete it. He gave them hope in their darkest hours. Guiding each student down his or her chosen path, he held their hand and became available to them. Why? It was his purpose.

As we discuss the pursing God, we are faced with his resurrection. The resurrection of Jesus from the dead is monumental. Many prophets had come and gone, but not one of them was able to be raised from the grave. Jesus' resurrection became the beacon of light that would provide hope for those who sought God. If Jesus could be raised from the dead, so can his followers. The pursing God truly is the "resurrection and the life" (John 11:25).

THE RESURRECTION OF JESUS

John 20:1-10 tells of the resurrection of Jesus from the dead. In a tomb with soldiers guarding him, there is plenty of eye witness testimony to his coming back from the dead. This story begins on the first day of the week, our Sunday, when Mary came to the tomb of Jesus. They took the body of Jesus from the cross on Friday in order to place him in the tomb before the holy Sabbath began. On Sunday, Mary approached the tomb at dawn and found that the enormous stone sealing the tomb was pushed away, and there was no body to be found within. Jesus had predicted that he would rise from the dead on the third day (Matt.16:21).

Mary turned around at the sight of the empty tomb and ran to Simon Peter and another follower of God, the apostle John. Believing someone stole Jesus' body, she declared what had happened, and the three of them returned to the tomb. Upon arrival, they found the linen and the face cloth folded in place. Following this event, John 20:11-16 tells us that Jesus appeared to Mary as she wept. After this appearance, Mary went and told the other followers of Jesus that she had seen him. That evening Jesus showed himself to the other followers and spoke with them.

It is important to know that the Jews and Romans took seriously the statement that Jesus would rise from the grave after three days. Matthew 27:62-66 shows how serious the Jewish leaders were about making sure Jesus did not have a following after his death. It teaches that guards, Roman soldiers, were hired to stand outside of the tomb in order to ensure nobody would be able to steal his body during the night. In addition to the soldiers, there was a seal placed on the stone in order to prove it had not been broken. Matthew 28:11-15 shares the rumor that was spread once Jesus had risen from the grave. Here the Jewish leaders paid the soldiers to tell people that the body of Jesus had been stolen as they slept rather than the true story of what happened. They even guaranteed the soldiers that if the Roman governor heard of this, they would help him stay out of trouble. A Roman soldier who lost a prisoner on his guard would often take the place of the prisoner that was lost.

THE IMPLICATION OF THE RESURRECTION

Each Easter Sunday, millions tune in as ministers preach the message of Jesus' resurrection. They learn the hope and guidance provided by the resurrection even in the darkest of night and that life, purpose, and reconciliation with God becomes possible through the resurrection. It serves as a demonstration of the ability to be forgiven of our sins and allows us to lay claim to our position in the family of God. The resurrection is life-giving.

Hope is a powerful word. In counseling, many walk into the office feeling hopeless. They feel as though there is no point to life, and even if there were, it is futile to strive for it. Their world is filled with chaos and misery. Sin has created a world that exhausts and defeats us. The concept of hope is often saved for a new car, dream home, or something material. As we pursue God, however, we set our hope towards heaven and the resurrection of Jesus that is promised to those who commit to him. This hope guides our lives and empowers us to stay the course as we chase after the creative God.

A resurrection also offers a new way to live life. Death and sin no longer lay claim to our lives. We are no longer separated from God by our old self because we have been raised to live a new life. This means all those sins that we struggle with no longer control us. Our blinders are on and focused on the task at hand.

This new direction of life comes with a renewed purpose of reconciliation. Just as Jesus instructed the disciples to go to all who will listen, baptize them, and teach them to obey his teachings, we are called to the same purpose. What is that purpose, specifically? It is the purpose of reconciling others to the pursuing God. We are in the business of reconciliation. 2 Corinthians 5:14-6:2 hammers this point in. We are called to be Jesus' ambassadors on earth as we proclaim the message he has given us and seek to bring others into reconciliation with God.

THE RESURRECTION AND LIFE

How are you living your life right now? What do you place your hope into? The world has much confusion about the purpose of life and what brings fulfillment. The pursuit of God is often viewed as a chore rather than something that gives life. Nothing could be further from the truth.

John 10:10 is a record of Jesus' declaration, "I came that they may have life and have it abundantly." There is no more powerful picture of this truth than the resurrection. Being reborn from the grave illustrates a strong ending and a new beginning. It shares a glimmer of light in a dark world and the hope of a new life. The resurrection in all its greatness did not come free; it cost the life of our savior. The pursuing God gave up everything to remove the wall between him and his creation. In what seemed to be the end of a grand rescue attempt, God saved the best news for last—a new life made possible through resurrection from death. It is because of Jesus' defeat of death that we can defeat death in the waters of baptism. The resurrected God provides victory over death.

SUMMARY

- You were created very good.
- God loves you enough to let you choose.
- Humanity betrayed God in sin.
- Betrayal frustrated and grieved God.
- Sin separates us from God and must be dealt with.

- God longs for our reconciliation.
- We pursue God as he pursues us.
- Our creator is merciful and welcoming.
- Jesus came to teach us to seek God.
- Jesus was tortured and murdered so we could find forgiveness.
- The resurrected God provides us victory over death.

QUESTIONS

1. What significance do you see in the resurrection?
2. How does a follower of Jesus live a resurrected life?
3. How are we to bury our old self so that we too can be raised to new life?
4. What is the resurrected God calling you to do?

CHAPTER TWELVE

THE RESTORING GOD

JOHN 20-21
ACTS 2:14-47

Imagine the most stressful time in your life where you needed your friends the most. During the trial and crucifixion of Jesus, Peter denied his friend and teacher. Luke 22 records that he denied knowing Jesus not only once, but three times. After doing this, Peter felt guilty and struggled with what had happened. Peter was the guy who said he would never deny knowing Jesus (Mark 14:31), but hard circumstances proved a different story.

JESUS APPEARS TO PETER

After Jesus appeared to some of the disciples, John 21:15-19 depicts his appearance to the apostle Peter. Three times Jesus asked Peter if he loved him more than anyone else. He was asking Peter if he was willing to put him, God, above anything and anyone else. Three times Peter affirmed this. Each affirmation was met with a directive from Jesus. In John 21:15 Jesus tells Peter to feed the sheep, then he instructs him to take care of the sheep (21:16), and he finishes by encouraging Peter to once again feed his sheep (21:17). Peter was asked to go about the work of Jesus, to continue what Jesus had begun. He was encouraged to live life the way that Jesus had modeled. John 21:18-19 shows the extent of Peter's following; he would be crucified like Jesus as a martyr on the cross.

How would you respond if God told you that he has restored you to his family, but you must carry on his work, even if faced with death? The restoring God called Peter to a work that was difficult but rewarding. You may not know how you will transition from this world to the next, but you are told that there is work to be done regardless of how it happens. What do we allow to distract us from the task of being restored and restoring others to God?

THE RESTORING GOD

In the book of Acts, Luke begins by painting the picture of Jesus' ascent into Heaven. In Acts 1:8, Jesus promises the Holy Spirit, who will remain with those who follow him until he returns. The second chapter of Acts brings the Holy Spirit that Jesus promised those who followed him. This Spirit would be with God's followers and give them understanding and a helper as they pursue him. It is during this time that Peter stood before a large crowd of people and began to share the story of the pursuing God. As Peter discloses the ultimate act of betrayal and separation from God, the crowd makes known their desire to be restored to their creator and Peter pleads for their restoration.

Think of a time you desired to press a "do over" button. When have you wished you could restore yourself to someone you have wronged? What about with someone who has wronged you? A child is given a time-out for an appropriate length of time before she may be restored to the family and activities at hand. The purpose of the time-out is not to permanently dismiss the child, but to restore the child to the family. The creative God does not desire to see those he created suffer; he desires to see them restored to him. God may allow suffering in order to encourage our return to the pursuit of him. Consequences are a natural part of discipline and restoration. Once we realize the need to be restored to God, how do we begin the process?

THE FIRST STEP TO RESTORATION

As followers of God seek to be restored to his family, they must begin by pursuing repentance. Repentance shows itself through genuine personal grief because one has done something against God, not sadness over getting caught or being punished. A child who is forced to apologize does it because he has been caught. This apology does not always lead to a change in heart and action. Things will be better for a while, but the habit will eventually find its way back into the child's life. This is known as worldly sorrow.

Second Corinthians 7:8-11 discusses the two types of sorrow that God sees. Worldly sorrow is a regret that one was caught in the act and now must pay a penalty. While a healthy dose of this is not bad, God desires those who pursue him to move beyond this view. According to Paul, godly sorrow consists of an attitude that is regretful of having wronged the individual. It is an internal regret and desire to right the wrong. In a world where it is easy to get petty when we are caught with our hand in the cookie jar, God desires us to regret the decision to turn away from him, not only because it brings harm to us, but because it harms our relationship with him.

Repentance, a godly sorrow, is the first step of restoring your relationship with God. As you pursue the creator, you must realize the lengths he went to in pursuit of you, and the steps we must take to respond. God wants us to choose him but only out of our free-will desire to love him. He loves us so much that he removed every obstacle to restore us to his family. We must begin our journey toward God in repentance as we restore ourselves and others to him.

THE BUSINESS OF RESTORATION

As previously discussed, the hope we find in the resurrection restores us to God so that we can restore others to him. This restoration happens as we seek to reconcile God's masterpiece, humanity, to the artist. This is the calling of students who pursue God. Even when we are seeking God, we can still take others along for the journey in hopes that they too may be restored to him. What does this reconciliation look like in our life and the lives of others? The answer to this is found in Paul's letter to the city of Corinth in the New Testament. Specifically, read Paul's instruction in 2 Corinthians 5:14-6:2.

First, restoration means that we have a new life in Jesus (2 Cor. 4:14-15). As we have discussed, our old life is done away with and our new life becomes the focus. One of the biggest struggles as we pursue God is to cease the pursuit of things that have no place in the life of God's student. Things that are sinful, ungodly, and divisive should be expelled as we recognize their presence in our lives. Restoration involves allowing Jesus to direct our lives and placing the old self on the cross.

Second, restoration alters our perception of others. As God begins to restore our life, he also restores our eyes. Paul writes that we are to look at others, not as the world views them, but how God views them—a masterpiece he desperately pursues. Our view of this world changes as well. We no longer view the material as more important than the spiritual. A follower pursues the things of God (love, grace, forgiveness, teaching others, and maintaining focus) rather than those of the world (money, positions, and fame). Our eyes become set on the spiritual, not the material (2 Cor. 5:16-17).

Third, as our eyes become focused on the spiritual, we begin to realize the importance of restoring others to God. Matthew 28:18-20 describes the importance of seeking the spiritual well-being of others for those who follow Jesus. This directive has been passed down to all who pursue God, even to this day. In fact, the Bible teaches that we are called to be ready to given an answer for the hope that we believe in (1 Pet. 3:15). Not everyone who pursues God is called to teach from the front of an auditorium or a large group of people, but we each have people we know that we can share the pursuit of God with. We are called to teach others about the restoration God offers and how they can participate in it as well. The God who pursues us is a God who desires to restore all of creation to him.

SUMMARY

- You were created very good.
- God loves you enough to let you choose.
- Humanity betrayed God in sin.
- Betrayal frustrated and grieved God.
- Sin separates us from God and must be dealt with.
- God longs for our reconciliation.
- We pursue God as he pursues us.
- Our creator is merciful and welcoming.
- Jesus came to teach us to seek God.
- Jesus was tortured and murdered so we could find forgiveness.
- The resurrected God provides us victory over death.
- God longs for you to be restored to him.

QUESTIONS

1. What is the difference between worldly and godly sorrow? List some examples.
2. How can you help others be restored to God?
3. Describe the lengths God went to so as to restore humanity to himself.
4. How are restoration and repentance (godly sorrow) related?
5. As Jesus restored Peter, how does he restore yet challenge us today?

CHAPTER THIRTEEN

THE WAITING GOD

MATTHEW 28:18-20
ROMANS 6:1-7

God has destined my adult life to be a continued development of patience. I live in a home with my wife and two daughters. My time is spent waiting on one of them at any given moment to do any given task. It does not matter how much planning or preparation takes place, you will find me waiting somewhere and running behind schedule. Brad Paisley sings a song about this called "Waiting on a Woman." All of us wait for something. God is no different. My patience is imperfect, but God's is perfect. God patiently waits for all of creation to be reconciled with him.

The God who pursues also waits for creation to return to him. God is ready and waiting to forgive you. He desires to make himself available to you. On a cross, Jesus died a horrible, cruel death to right the wrongs that drove a wedge between God and humanity. Crime requires penalty, so God provided a scapegoat to take on our penalty, much like a father would take a bullet for his child.

This same God is now waiting for you to pursue him. He yearns to hear your prayers and do away with your sin. God will do everything possible to reach you but freedom of choice dictates that you must also reach out to him. As parents anxiously await the birth of their child, the creator awaits your return. How does one begin to pursue the waiting God? Where does the journey home begin?

Chasing God includes listening to his instruction, and then acting upon it. Before we can begin to walk with God, we must deal with the sin that separates us from his presence. God provided a means to overcome the sin problem. While Jesus physically took up his cross, we must do so spiritually. This is accomplished in what is called baptism.

WHAT HAPPENS IN BAPTISM

We hear many things about baptism but often struggle to find answers to our questions concerning what happens during the process of baptism. It is true that the immersion into water is symbolic and an outward display of what is happening in the spirit, but the Bible says there are specific things that happen when one is baptized in water that do not happen beforehand. Romans 6:1-7 offers a beautiful picture of what baptism does. Let's turn our focus to this passage in order to find three things that take place during baptism.

First, Paul tells the Roman church that baptism brings about forgiveness of sins. Paul discourages the erroneous pattern of thought that after we have been forgiven, we are free to live however we desire. Rather, Paul says that when we are baptized, we are buried with him in death (as we go under the water). Soon after Jesus returned to Heaven, the apostle Peter speaks to a crowd of people about Jesus and shares the story of God. At the conclusion of Peter's sermon, the crowd begs Peter to direct them in how to respond to this pursuit of God. Peter's answer is found in Acts 2:38, "And Peter said to them, 'Repent and be baptized every one of you in the name of Jesus Christ *for* the forgiveness of your sins, and you will receive the gift of the Holy Spirit.'" Did you notice the word that I italicized? The word "for" in this context means "in order to receive." This directive indicates that baptism brings about forgiveness as we are set free from our sinfulness. In fact, Jesus illustrated the saving nature of baptism for us as it is recorded in Mark 16:16, "Whoever believes and is baptized will be saved, but whoever does not believe will be condemned." The immersion of water brings freedom from sin according to Jesus and Paul, but that is not all it does.

The second action that takes place during baptism is that we are born into a new family. Romans 6:1-7 reminds us that those who obey God in baptism are buried into death with Christ, where our sins are forgiven. In his letter to the church in Corinth, Greece, Paul adds to this understanding of baptism. In 1 Corinthians 12:13, Paul writes, "For in one Spirit we were all baptized into one body—Jews or Greeks, slaves or free—and all were made to drink of one Spirit." Those who are baptized are brought together into a new body. They are born into a family of God. No longer do we have to wade through sin and this temporal world alone. A new family awaits those who put Christ on in baptism to pursue God alongside them.

The coming of the Spirit of God is the third thing that takes place in baptism. Looking back at Acts 2:38, Peter suggests that baptism brings about the Spirit of God. This was made evident all the way back at the baptism of Jesus. As Jesus comes up from the water, the Bible says the Spirit [of God] rested upon him. God's Spirit is found throughout the entire Bible. In the Old Testament we see it as God begins his creative work. Various kings, prophets, and others were given God's Spirit in the stories of the Old Testament. There is, however, a significant difference between the Spirit's occurrences in the Old and New Testaments. While the Spirit came and went among various individuals in the Old Testament, the instances were temporary and selective. The New Testament teaches that anyone who is immersed in baptism receives the Spirit of God in his or her life. In baptism, it does not come for only a temporary time; rather, it makes its home within you and stays with you for the duration of your pursuit of God.

Finally, baptism brings about a new life in you. Romans 6:4-5 teaches that in baptism, we are raised to walk in a new life and will be given a resurrection like that of Jesus. This means new Christians must continually remind themselves that their old selves have been done away with, and they have made a conscious choice to live a new, different kind of life. It is a life focused on pursuing God and teaching others to do so as well. Paul writes in 2 Corinthians 5:17, "Therefore, if anyone is in Christ, he is a new creation. The old has passed away; behold, the new has come." We have a new direction, a higher calling. The purpose and challenge God has given us as we pursue him includes an examination of what must be let go of so we can cling to him. A man once said, "The old Irish, when immersing a person at baptism, left out the right arm so that it would remain pagan for good fighting." Although comical, this is not the attitude a Christian should take. Jesus called us to deal radically with sin. God waits for us with open arms, but our pursuit of him necessitates a change in our life and ways.

THE FATHER'S INVITATION

The story of the runaway son in Luke 15:11-32 reminds us of the patience and longing a loving father has for the return of his lost child. The creative God who formed you in his likeness holds many similarities to the father in Luke 15. God pursues you, yet he also waits for you to choose him. He longs to be reconciled with you, to help you overcome the separation caused by sin. Second Timothy 1:4 teaches that God desires all people to be saved and come to the knowledge of truth. That includes you! God desperately wants a relationship with you and goes out of his way to achieve that. However, a God who creates freedom of choice cannot force you to choose him. He longs for your pursuit but leaves the choice to you.

The Ethiopian eunuch in Acts 8:36 declared, "See, here is water! What prevents me from being baptized?" He desired to pursue and obey the wonderful creator of humanity. There was a sense of immediacy as the eunuch learned what was asked of him and how to begin his journey with God. The same question is asked of you. What keeps you from being baptized? What holds you back from pursuing the creative God who loves you and runs towards you? We are not guaranteed tomorrow (Jas. 4:13-17). Today is the day God calls you to make a choice. How will you respond to the God who pursues you?

THE WAITING GOD

God waits for creation to be reconciled to him. Baptism is only one step in that direction, but it is a vital step, a first step. We cannot approach God until our sin is dealt with. May God bless you as you pursue him and encourage others to do the same.

SUMMARY

- You were created very good.
- God loves you enough to let you choose.
- Humanity betrayed God in sin.
- Betrayal frustrated and grieved God.
- Sin separates us from God and must be dealt with.
- God longs for our reconciliation.
- We pursue God as he pursues us.
- Our creator is merciful and welcoming.
- Jesus came to teach us to seek God.
- Jesus was tortured and murdered so we could find forgiveness.
- The resurrected God provides us victory over death.
- God longs for you to be restored to him.
- God has pursued you and now waits for your response. What will you choose?

QUESTIONS

1. Throughout these chapters, how would you explain the overall story of the pursuing God to someone?

2. What does God wait patiently for? Why is he waiting for it?

3. After all God has been through on your behalf, how does his example provide a model for your Christian life?

4. What is achieved at baptism, and why is it vital to someone seeking God?

5. If you have not been baptized as shown in the Bible, what keeps you from obeying? What hurdles might you face in obeying this teaching?

6. If you are already baptized, what decision do you need to make to get closer to God today?

APPENDIX A

THE APPROACH

ABOUT THE APPROACH

This course is called "Pursuing God" and can be taught to both non-Christians or reviewed with a new Christian. The goals are to get each student of Christ to:

1. Look closely at the Word of God

2. Understand and Remember what is going on in the text

3. Do what the text teaches (Jas. 1:21-25)

It is intended primarily as an evangelistic study that not only shares the story of God's pursuit, but also teaches the reader how to study the Bible and implement its timeless teachings. As one author wrote, "We want to become architects of passion and purpose." This course is designed to begin that journey as you help your friends understand their purpose and instill a passion to fulfill it. My experience teaches that if the facilitator can lead the student to rely upon the Word of God and his own reasoning ability, the student will not only fall in love with God, but will be eager to obey his teachings with a willing heart.

This study is designed to be self-directed and requires little reliance upon the "teacher" or discussion leader. I actually prefer the term facilitator as we are guides pointing our friend in a direction rather than an expert on the matter at hand. For this reason, rather than relying upon the teacher for expertise, the student is taught to rely upon the Bible. The facilitator is there to help the student find answers to any additional questions and to keep the conversation moving. He or she also functions as someone who helps to hold the student accountable to the implementation of Biblical truth in his or her life as he/she finds it. While this is usually contrary to what we have been taught, part of being architects of passion and purpose involves letting go of control and learning how to release people. We must help each of our friends learn how to stand on his or her own and "work out his/her own salvation" while we offer guidance and gentle correction. This study is the first step in helping our friends walk before they run.

THE METHOD

In the very nature of this study, it becomes obvious that a facilitator is there to guide the discussion while the student dives into the Bible in search for precious gems of applicable wisdom and understanding. It must be understood that this is not a lecture format and should not be treated as such. We should also be careful not to be too quick to rescue a student who is struggling with a text. Provide the student some room to grapple with a text or concept before interjecting. You might be amazed at how often the student will find the correct answer if given a moment to wrestle with the passage. Following are some helpful tips and general guidance as to how one might carry out a session.

ITEMS NEEDED

1. The study
2. Pen or pencil

3. Two Bibles (in case your friend does not own one)

4. An observer (it's always good to take someone with you who can learn how to study with a friend)

5. White board (if desired)

PARTS OF THE STUDY GUIDE

The Overview. At the top of each guide, you will see the series name and lesson title followed by the objectives, Scriptures covered, and assigned homework. The facilitator will discuss only those passages labeled under "Scriptures" while those labeled "At Home" are to be done by the student on his/her own to encourage further growth outside of your meeting. This results in helping establish a personal Bible study habit. Another way to hold this study is to start with the "My Salvation Journey" sheet in the first session and then have the student complete one lesson a week prior to arriving at the study. This allows more time for processing information at home and discussion of questions and concerns in your time together.

On Your Own. These sections usually contain many of the questions discussed with the group as well as additional questions to be considered at home. These questions are to be answered on the sheet and brought back at the next meeting time.

Next Meeting. At the end of each sheet there is a place to write when the group will meet next including the time, date, and place. It is very important to fill this out before anyone leaves.

Prayer & Share. At the end of lesson one there are three blanks to encourage each student to write down the names of those he/she wants to share his/her findings with. This is to provide an avenue into learning how to pray for people as well as preparing the student to share the Words of Life with others. By placing this in the first lesson, the student is already being taught, from day one, about God's expectation for us to become a light in the darkness.

BEGINNING THE STUDY

Group Interaction—Check in with your group. Ask how the week went and what happened that can be prayed for.

Prayer—Begin in prayer and specifically mention any thanksgivings, concerns, and struggles that came up in discussion. If others are comfortable, allow them to say their prayer as well.

Review Last Lesson (if applicable)—Find out what they learned last week and how they are doing at being accountable to God. Express the expectation of change by asking what changes in behavior or thought last week's lesson brought about in their life. Make sure they understand that they are not alone, and we are all here to help each other pursue God and love him as he loves us!

Sharing Reports—Ask how it went throughout the week telling their friends about the study and what they are learning from the Word of God. Ask if God has opened any doors to share with others in their lives. Sharing these experiences provides support, accountability, expectation, new ideas, and encouragement.

Open the Bible—It is now time to explain the study of the week. Begin by having them turn to the selected passage and move through the facilitator and at home guide.

Close with a Plan—End with plans for sharing the study throughout the next week and set up the place, time, and date of your next meeting before anyone leaves.

COURSE
OVERVIEW

LESSON 1: GOD CREATES MAN

Objectives:

- To understand humanity was created as good.
- To understand God loves and provides for our needs.
- To understand that God gave us the freedom of choice.

Scriptures: Genesis 2:4-25

At Home: Genesis 1:1-31

LESSON 2: SIN AND ITS ORIGIN

Objectives:

- Sin is choosing our desires over those of God.
- Sin has consequences.
- Sin comes from our own evil intentions.

Scriptures: Genesis 3:1-13, 14-24; 6:5-8; Mark 7:14-23

At Home: Galatians 5:19-21

LESSON 3: EFFECTS OF OUR SIN

Objectives:

- To understand that sin severs our relationship with God.
- To understand how sin personally impacts our lives.
- To understand we must deal radically with our sins.

Scriptures: Isaiah 59:1-2; Romans 7:13-25; Matthew 5:27-30

At Home: James 1:12-15

LESSON 4: GOD'S DESIRE FOR US

Objectives:

- To demonstrate God's desire to bless us.
- To understand how one obtains God's blessing.
- To learn how to actively seek God in our daily lives.

Scriptures: Jeremiah 29:11-14; Acts 17:26-27; 8:26-40

At Home: Matthew 13:44-46

LESSON 5: GOD TAKES SIN PERSONALLY

Objectives:

- To understand that God sought to deal personally with sin.
- To realize the love God has for us.

- To begin looking at the example set by God.

Scriptures: Luke 2:1-21; Mark 1:9-11; Matthew 4:1-11

At Home: Luke 15:1-32; Matthew 18:10-14

LESSON 6: GOD ASKS US TO FOLLOW HIM

Objectives:

- To learn how to follow God.
- To understand the seriousness of our commitment to God.
- To answer the call of God.

Scriptures: Luke 6:39-40; 9:23-26, 57-62

At Home: Luke 14:25-27; John 8:31-32; Matthew 28:18-20

LESSON 7: GOD DEALS WITH SIN

Objectives:

- To understand the consequences of sin.
- To realize the enormous love God has for us.
- To explain the hope found in the resurrection.

Scriptures: Isaiah 53; Luke 23; Luke 24

At Home: Matthew 28

LESSON 8: GOD RESTORES HIS FAMILY (YOU)

Objectives:

- To seek out the gifts and provisions of God.

- To understand our response to and acceptance of God.
- To commit ourselves to God on his terms.

Scriptures: Luke 13:1-5; Acts 2:36-41; 21:40-22:16

At Home: 2 Corinthians 7:8-11; Acts 22:16

BIBLE EXPLORATION GUIDE

MY SALVATION JOURNEY

MY CURRENT UNDERSTANDING OF MY SALVATION

1. How were you saved? How old were you?

2. While we are saved by God's grace, what actions did you take to accept that salvation?

3.   At what point during the process were you saved (e.g. when I said a prayer, when I was sprinkled, when I committed myself to listening to the church)?

4.   Were you baptized? If so, how were you baptized (e.g. sprinkled with water, as an infant, immersed in water, said a prayer)?

5.   At what point did you receive the Holy Spirit?

6.   When did God forgive all of your sins?

GOD CREATES MAN

OBJECTIVES

- To understand humanity was created as good.
- To understand God loves and provides for our needs.
- To understand that God gave us the freedom of choice.

ON YOUR OWN

Read Genesis 2:4-25

1. Whether good or bad, what stuck out to you in this passage?

2.   Do you have any questions? Is there anything you're struggling to understand?

3.   Why do you think God created man?

4.   According to the Bible, why did God create the woman?

5.   Genesis 2:25 says, "They were not ashamed of being naked." Why do you think the author pointed this out?

6.   What does this passage tell us about God's view of humanity in the beginning?

7.   How did God provide for the needs of the man and woman?

8. Re-read Genesis 2:16-17. What significance do these verses have on our understanding of humanity's freedom of choice?

9. What does this passage teach you to do? Using sentences beginning with "I will..." write down the actions this passage calls you to do. For example, you might say, "I will trust that God made me good."

Read Genesis 1:1-31

1. How did God feel about his creation according to the Bible?

2. What does it mean to be created in the image of something or someone?

3. Who was humanity created in the image of?

4.   Genesis 1:28 reads, "God blessed them [humans]." How did he bless them?

5.   How does this passage relate to the previous one (Gen. 2:4-24)?

6.   What do you find most interesting in this section?

7.   What additional questions do you have?

8.   What does this passage teach you to do? Using sentences beginning with "I will..." write down the actions this passage calls you to take. For example, you might say, "I will enjoy God's blessings."

I'm so glad we were able to study together. Every time I read these passages, I see something new and interesting that I missed the last time. Please review this lesson between now and the next time we meet together. Bring this back with you so that we can discuss any further questions or insights you have.

We all have people in our lives that might be interested in hearing and learning from these stories. Think of three people you can start sharing our lessons with and write their names on the bottom of this sheet.

1. _____

2. _____

3. _____

Next Meeting Day, Time, and Place: _____

SIN AND ITS ORIGIN

OBJECTIVES

- Sin is choosing our desires over those of God.
- Sin has consequences.
- Sin comes from our own evil intentions.

ON YOUR OWN

Read Genesis 3:1-24

1. What caught your attention in this passage? Explain.

2. What does this story teach us about humanity (ourselves)?

3. Why do you think Adam and Eve disobeyed God?

4. How did their sin impact the relationship they had with God and their innocence?

5. What does this passage teach you to do? Using sentences beginning with "I
will..." write down the actions this passage calls you to take.

Read Genesis 6:5-10

1. What do you think it means when the text says, "it grieved God to his heart?"

2.   Why do you think God was upset with humanity?

3.   What made Noah different from all the other humans?

4.   What does this passage teach you to do? What lessons does it hold for you and me? Using sentences beginning with "I will..." write down the actions this passage calls you to take. For example, you might say, "I will follow Noah's example."

Read Mark 7:14-23

1.   What is the main point of Jesus' teaching in this section?

2.   What does this teach about sin?

3. How does this relate to the story of Adam and Eve's sin? What caused their sin?

4. What are some sins you can think of that "come from the heart?"

5. What does this passage teach you to do? Using sentences beginning with "I will..." write down the actions this passage calls you to take.

Read Galatians 5:19-21

1. What questions do you have about this passage?

2. How does this selection relate to our current study and relationship to God?

3. We all struggle with sin, which of these listed sins do you find yourself struggling with?

4. What do you struggle with in the passage? What does this passage teach you to do? Using sentences beginning with "I will…" write down the actions this passage calls you to take. For example, you might say, "I will stop being jealous."

5. In reviewing your action items, what must you do this week in order to make these a reality and obey the Bible?

Next Meeting Day, Time, and Place: _____

Please review this lesson between now and the next time we meet together. Bring back with you so that we can discuss any further questions or insights you have.

EFFECTS OF SIN

OBJECTIVES

- To understand that sin severs our relationship with God.
- To understand how sin personally impacts our lives.
- To understand we must deal radically with our sins.

ON YOUR OWN

Read Isaiah 59:1-2

1. What sticks out to you as interesting from this passage?

2. What do these verses tell us about the separation between us and God?

3. Why does God not hear or help some people? Does he want to help them?

4. In thinking back to Genesis 1-2, how does this relate to Adam and Eve?

5. What does this passage teach you to do? Using sentences beginning with "I will..." write down the actions this passage calls you to take.

Read Romans 7:13-25

1. What did you find interesting? Do you have any questions about these verses?

2. Robert Cox shares how this passage teaches five ways sin impacts our lives:

    1) Sin enslaves me (v. 14)

    2) Sin confuses me (v. 15)

    3) Sin steals my confidence (vv. 18-19)

    4) Sin condemns me (vv. 23-24)

    5) Sin calls me to make a choice (v. 25)

3. How do Robert's points relate to Adam and Eve? What about to you?

4. What does this passage teach you to do? Using sentences beginning with "I will..." write down the actions this passage calls you to practice.

Read Matthew 5:27-30

1. What does this teach us about sin and its impact on the relationship between us and God?

2.   What is the main point of this passage?

3.   How are we to deal with sin that is in our lives? Why?

4.   What does this passage teach you to do? Using sentences beginning with "I will…" write down the actions this passage calls you to implement.

Read James 1:12-15

1.   What questions do you have about this passage?

2.   How does this selection relate to our current study and the severing of our relationship with God?

3. Thinking back to the previous lesson, what does this say about the passage in Galatians 5:19-21?

4. If we deal radically with our sin, if we purge it from our lives, what will the reward be according to this passage?

5. Using sentences beginning with "I will..." write down the actions this passage calls you to take.

6. In reviewing your action items, what must you do this week in order to make those a reality and obey Scripture?

Next Meeting Day, Time, and Place: _____

Please review this lesson between now and the next time we meet together. Bring this back with you so that we can discuss any further questions or insights you may have.

LESSON 4

GOD'S DESIRE FOR US

OBJECTIVES:

- To demonstrate God's desire to bless us.
- To understand how one obtains God's blessing.
- To learn how to actively seek God in our daily lives.

ON YOUR OWN:

Read Jeremiah 29:11-14

1. According to Jeremiah, what does God want for your future?

2.   What promises and conditions do you see in vv. 12-14?

3.   What are signs that a person is seeking something with "all of his/her heart?"

4.   What does this tell us about God's love for us when compared with Genesis 1-2?

5.   What does this passage teach you to do? Using sentences beginning with "I will..." write down the actions this passage calls you to take.

Read Acts 17:26-27

1.   What intrigues you about this passage? What questions do you have?

2. What does this passage teach about God's relationship with humans?

3. What do you think the point of this passage is? How does it relate to our study about God's desire for and pursuit of us?

4. What does this passage teach you to take? Using sentences beginning with "I will..." write down the actions this passage calls you to implement.

Read Acts 8:26-40

1. What do you find interesting in this passage?

2. How do we know the Ethiopian was seeking after God?

3. How did the Ethiopian respond to God's desire for him? Why is the eunuch a good illustration of Jeremiah 29:11-14?

4. What does this passage teach you to do? Using sentences beginning with "I will..." write down the actions this passage encourages you to do.

Read Matthew 13:44-46

1. What questions do you have about this passage?

2. How does this selection relate to our current study and the response to God's desire for us?

3. What does this teach us about the treasures of God (or Kingdom of Heaven)?

4.   How much did the treasure cost the man? Why would he take such action?

5.   Using sentences beginning with "I will..." write down the actions this passage calls you to take.

6.   In reviewing your action items, what must you do this week in order to make those a reality and obey Scripture?

Next Meeting Day, Time, and Place: _____

Please review this lesson between now and the next time we meet together. Bring this back with you so that we can discuss any further questions or insights you may have.

GOD TAKES SIN PERSONALLY

OBJECTIVES:

- To understand that God sought to deal personally with sin.
- To realize the love God has for us.
- To begin looking at the example set by God.

ON YOUR OWN:

Read Luke 2:1-21

1. What do you find interesting in this passage?

2.   What does the angel mean in v. 11 by the word "Savior?"

3.   Why do you think God loved us so much that he came to earth to live as one of us?

4.   What does this passage teach you to do?

Read Mark 1:9-11

1.   How was Jesus baptized (look to v. 10 for help)?

2.   When did the Holy Spirit come upon Jesus?

3.   When did God announce his pleasure with Jesus?

4. What does this passage teach you to do? It may help to think of what examples Jesus sets for us in this verse.

Read Matthew 4:1-11

1. What do you find interesting in this passage?

2. How does Jesus teach us to answer the temptations of the devil?

3. When considering where sin comes from (remember back to lessons 2 and 3), what do we have to do in order to resist temptation?

4. What does this passage teach you to do? Using sentences beginning with "I will…" write down the actions this passage calls you to practice.

Read Luke 15:1-32

1. How does this relate to our current study and the love God has for us, his creation?

2. How did the son sin against his father and family?

3. What did it take for the son to gain forgiveness from his father?

4. What example does the father set for us?

5. Using sentences beginning with "I will..." write down the actions this passage calls you to take.

Read Matthew 18:12-14

1. How does this selection relate to our current study and the love of God?

2. How does this relate to our study about the pursuit of God?

3. What is the will of God for humanity (look in v. 14)?

4. In reviewing your action items, what must you do this week in order to make those a reality and obey Scripture?

Next Meeting Day, Time, and Place: _____

Please review this lesson between now and the next time we meet together. Bring this back with you so that we can discuss any further questions or insights you might have.

GOD ASKS US TO FOLLOW HIM

OBJECTIVES:

- To learn how to follow God.
- To understand the seriousness of our commitment to God.
- To answer the call of God.

ON YOUR OWN:

Read Luke 6:39-40

1. What makes a good student (one who is fully trained)?

2.   How does this apply to pursuing God?

3.   What does this passage teach you to do?

Read Luke 9:23-26, 57-62

1.   What is Jesus asking a follower to commit to?

2.   What does it mean to deny oneself?

3.   In what ways do you need to deny yourself as you pursue God?

4. What is the point of Luke 9:57-62, and how does it relate to our study?

5. Robert Cox points out that Jesus wants three things when it comes to pursuing him:

    1) That you accept the difficulties of following Christ (v. 58)

    2) That you let nothing stop you from sharing your faith (v. 60)

    3) That you are serious about leaving your old life (v. 62)

6. What do these passages teach you to do?

Read Luke 14:25-27

1. What is the main point Jesus is getting at in this passage?

2. Why do you think Jesus wants you to love him more than anything else?

3. What does this passage teach you to do?

Read John 8:31-32

1. From this passage, what must you do to really be a disciple?

2. What does it mean to "hold on to his teachings" or "abide in his word"?

3. What happens when you hold on to the teachings (words) of Jesus?

4. Using sentences beginning with "I will..." write down the actions this passage encourages you to take.

Read Matthew 28:18-20

1. What were the disciples told to teach others to do?

2. According to this passage, how were people to respond to Jesus' teachings?

3. Using sentences beginning with "I will..." write down the actions this passage calls you to take.

4. In reviewing your action items, what must you do this week in order to make those a reality and obey Scripture?

Next Meeting Day, Time, and Place: _____

Please review this lesson between now and the next time we meet together. Bring this back with you so that we can discuss any further questions or insights you have.

GOD DEALS WITH SIN

OBJECTIVES:

- To understand the consequences of our sin.
- To realize the enormous love God has for us.
- To explain the hope found in the resurrection.

ON YOUR OWN:

Read Isaiah 53

1. Isaiah 53 is a prediction of what will happen to Jesus. Why was Jesus wounded and punished?

2.   According to Isaiah 53:5-6 and 53:12, what were some of the benefits this punishment brought to God's people?

3.   What does this passage teach you to do? Using sentences beginning with "I will..." write down the actions this passage calls you to take.

Read Luke 23

1.   What did you find interesting in this chapter?

2.   Why do you think Pilate gave Jesus up to be crucified?

3.   Based upon all we've studied so far, why was it so important for Jesus to give his life on a cross?

4.   What do you think about Jesus' words in Luke 23:34?

5.   What do these passages teach you to take?

Read Luke 24

1.   From this chapter, what do we learn about God's plan for humans?

2.   Why was it so hard for some to believe Jesus rose from the dead?

3.   Why does the passage say that the Christ had to die and rise from death?

4. What was their response to seeing Jesus alive again and his going back into heaven?

5. What does this passage teach you to do? Using sentences beginning with "I will..." write down the actions that this passage calls you to do.

Read Matthew 28

1. What were the disciples told to teach others to do?

2. According to this passage, how were people to respond to Jesus' teachings?

3. What are students of Jesus supposed to teach?

4. Earlier we discussed that we are to follow the example of Jesus, how does Jesus show baptism is accomplished?

5. What is the purpose of being baptized?

6. Using sentences beginning with "I will..." write down the actions this passage teaches you to practice.

7. In reviewing your action items, what must you do this week in order to make those a reality and obey Scripture?

Next Meeting Day, Time, and Place: _____

Please review this lesson between now and the next time we meet together. Bring this back with you so that we can discuss any further questions or insights you have.

GOD EXTENDS HIS GIFT TO YOU

OBJECTIVES:

- To seek out the gifts and provisions of God.
- To understand our response to and acceptance of God.
- To commit ourselves to God on his terms.

ON YOUR OWN:

Read Luke 13:1-5

1. How is someone restored to God according to this passage?

2.   What does it mean to repent?

3.   What is the consequence of not repenting?

4.   What does this passage teach you to do? Using sentences beginning with "I will..." write down the actions this passage calls you to take.

Read Acts 2:36-41

1.   What was Peter's reply when the crowd asked what they should do?

2.   What was promised if they did what Peter said?

3. Why do you think the crowd was convicted?

4. What do these passages teach you to do? Using sentences beginning with "I will..." write down the actions this passage calls you to take.

Read Acts 21:40-Acts 22:16

1. What struck you as interesting in this passage?

2. Why did Paul need to be baptized?

3. Why do you think baptism is so important in the life of a disciple?

4. What does this passage teach you to do? Using sentences beginning with "I will..." write down the actions this passage calls you to take.

Read 2 Corinthians 7:8-11

1. Paul mentions two kinds of grief (or sorrow). What are they?

2. What do you think is the difference between worldly and godly sorrow/grief?

3. With what words does Paul describe godly sorrow?

4. Which sorrow do you relate too and what is the Bible teaching you to do with it?

5. Using sentences beginning with "I will..." write down the actions this passage calls you to practice.

6. Are you ready to accept the gifts of God on His terms? Why?

7. When do you want to be immersed in water?

As we've studied the Pursuit of God, we have noted that not only does God desire a relationship with us, God went out of his way extending the gift of life and resurrection to you. According to Matthew 28:18-20 and Acts 22:16, one must be baptized for forgiveness and the acceptance of God's Holy Spirit. Baptism brings about these gifts of God. It is the biblical response to God's loving pursuit of us.

GOD'S SALVATION JOURNEY

WHAT DOES SCRIPTURE TEACHE ME ABOUT MY SALVATION?

1. Do your answers from your salvation journey page (p. 97) match what the Bible teaches?

2. Prior to searching the Bible, had you come to an understanding of your salvation by what Jesus has asked you to do or by what humans have asked you to do?

3.   If it is according to what humans have asked you to do, what must you do to pursue God on his terms?

4.   Is there anything you have not done that the Bible teaches leads to salvation? If so, what keeps you from doing it?

Made in United States
Orlando, FL
14 February 2022

14793168R00078